What others are saying about...

The Power of Humility

"I met Clay Mize when he showed up in my office unannounced, but I am glad that I took the time to get to know him. *The Power of Humility* will bless your life."–**Mark Richt, Head Football Coach, University of Georgia**

"*The Power of Humility* by Clay Mize is one of the best books I have ever read about making yourself happier. Practicing humility is a must if you want to be happy with yourself and admired by everyone." **–Steve Spurrier, Head Football Coach, University of South Carolina**

"Read this book written by Clay Mize on Humility. Humility is a virtue missing in American society today. All of the Apostles had it." **–Bobby Bowden, Former Head Football Coach, Florida State University**

"Pride and self absorbtion are very common in our culture. In *The Power of Humility*, Clay Mize offers a simple yet strong case for approaching life in a humble, appreciative walk with God." **–Tom Osborne, Athletic Director, University of Nebraska**

"I find that the most influential people in life serve others with great joy and hold firm to the idea of others before self. Clay Mize clearly points out steps to being an influential person that can be used by God in a mighty way in *The Power of Humility*." **–Hugh Freeze, Head Football Coach, University of Mississippi**

"The most powerful people I have ever met are the ones who possess that true humility that is a by-product of a consistent walk with God. You show me a happy heart and most times you will see a humble heart. Clay uses his life's experience to help us all find and stay on this path that truly honors the Lord."–**John Croyle, Founder of Big Oak Ranch, A Christian home for children needing a chance.**

"The attitude of 'being coachable' is the main ingredient to maximizing your development as an athlete. The same concept holds true in your spiritual development. Clay Mize helps us to realize that this attitude of being coachable stems from humility. Plain and simple, if you want to become everything God created you to be you must understand true humility and reading *The Power of Humility* is the perfect place to start."–**Rob Likens, Assistant Head Football Coach, University of California Berkeley**

"Jesus says the joy of living comes only to the 'poor in spirit.' In other words: I will never allow Jesus to manage my life until I see I am too spiritually 'poverty stricken' to manage it myself: Humility! In this book Clay Mize illustrates how such humility is the first step on our journey to joy." –**Lynn Anderson, Hope Network, Author of The Jesus Touch, and Finding the Heart to Go On**

"In Ephesians 4:1-2, we are taught that we are to walk in a manner worthy of our calling with all humility. Yet in our society, pride is not only accepted, but encouraged. In The Power of Humility, Clay Mize explains how humility is an essential ingredient in binding together the virtues of the Christian life. Only through humility can we love others like Christ first loved us. In this book, Clay demonstrates that with humility, we not only realize the fruits of Christ in our lives, but more importantly, in the lives of those surrounding us." –**Weston Smith, Former CFO HealthSouth Corporation**

"Good job, 'Coach' Clay Mize, for kindly taking us back to the fundamentals, the blocking and tackling of life. The most sublime teaching of the ages is not complicated, but I sure can lose it quick in the stressfulness of daily existence. I needed these gentle and thoughtful words." **–Randy Boggs, Elder at Oak Hills Church in San Antonio and First VP at Morgan Stanley Investments**

"Clay Mize has written a book that looks at the heart of humility. Many of us experience humility when we witness a baby's birth, or sit with a friend at their end of life. For others humility is being awed by nature, whether looking at a beautiful landscape, or the wrath of a storm. Humility also is present when we realize the sacrifices those who loved us willingly and freely gave for our benefit. The Universe, we are told, keeps expanding, and this appears to also mean that God is speaking to us all now, calling us to do our best for ourselves and for others as well, surrendering to a power we can hardly imagine, humbly. Join Clay and share his experiences as he writes about his continuing journey of discovery."-**Walter L. Blanchard, Ph.D.**

"Clay Mize has tapped into one of the cardinal virtues given in Scripture for one who would walk in the fullness of God. Clay's book, *The Power of Humility*, is easy to read, majors in practical application, and could be used effectively as a guide for a small group or Bible class. Having known Clay for over twenty years, we know that he is diligent in his pursuit of God. Your careful and prayerful reading of this book will help you in developing the grace of humility."**–Jim Bevis, President, Founder of CSR Ministries, Mid-South Directors PastorCare**

"*The Power of Humility* is a great resource for Sunday School teachers, small group leaders or business leaders. This book will lead to heart-to-heart conversations and push readers to think and grow. We all know that the one thing our country and culture could definitely use more of is...Humility. This book not only speaks to the absence of it in our time but also how to implement it back as a highly valued priority in our daily lives."– **Mark Maybrey, Minister at Macedonia Church of Christ, Florence, AL**

The Power of Humility

The Secret to Being Happy

Clay Mize

The Power of Humility

Published by Thorn Hill Books
117 Lakewood Drive
Sheffield, AL 35660

ISBN-13: 978-0615868486

ISBN-10: 0615868487

**THORN HILL
BOOKS**

To Gene and Ruth Mize

Acknowledgments

I would like to express my appreciation to my friends and mentors who have added such richness to my life. I love and appreciate my home town of Haleyville, AL, which gave me the confidence to believe that I could do anything. I also appreciate my new home of Florence, Sheffield, Tuscumbia and Muscle Shoals, AL, known collectively as The Shoals which is the most beautiful place on the earth, and has the finest people too.

I appreciate Devon Hester who listened to rewrites too numerous to count and encouraged me to keep going. I would like to thank Chandler Moseley, who inspires me to be bold and to ask God to give me more opportunities to help people. I would like to thank Anita Lyons, who helped with some of the early edits, Dr. Hardy who helped me believe I could be a writer, Paul Conant, my editor, for his dedication to the details, Leslie Gober my publicist for giving me a bigger vision, and finally, I appreciate those who took the time to endorse my work.

Above all I thank God for giving me the motivation and insight to write the book and the patience and endurance to complete it.

Contents

Part Four

How Humility will Make you Happier with your Community......... 145

Part Five

How Humility will Make you Happier with your World 181

The Power of Humility

The Secret to Being Happy

Introduction

B lessed or happy are the poor in spirit (The Humble) (Matt. 5:3). This famous quote by Jesus during his Sermon on the Mount always baffled me. It conjured in my mind a door mat...a person with low self-esteem and little confidence. It was the opposite of what I perceived was the truth about who is happy.

Did Jesus mean for a person to be happy he must be obscure, insignificant, irrelevant, and unimportant?

The following statement better fits my old way of looking at who is happy...Blessed are the rich, the powerful, the beautiful, and the intelligent for theirs is happiness on the earth.

Part of my reason for researching this topic was to understand why the humble are blessed. My quest for understanding this has led me to believe there are two types of humility. The first type of humility is one that is forged from difficult experiences. It is woven one stitch at a time with pain and struggle into the fabric of who a person is.

The impetus for this type of humility could be enduring the crushing grind of poverty or a limiting defect or disability. It could also come from the stigma of being the wrong color, having the wrong address or belonging to a parent serving time.

This type of humility cannot be taught, for it is only learned the hard way. In a way this type of humility is still a choice. The person who endures this type of suffering could choose anger or bitterness, instead of humility, as many do. In these circumstances, to choose humility is to choose the grace of God, and in time, the grace of God always makes beauty out of ashes.

A person who exudes this type of humility is attractive to me. There is an aroma about them that draws me in and causes me to want to know them better. I genuinely desire to know their story, learn from them and to understand how choosing grace has impacted them.

Though I am tempted to emulate such a person, I realize the road to this type of humility is no easy path, and one I would not choose if I fully understood the price paid for it.

We will focus on the other type of humility in this book. It too is attractive and it can be taught and learned. You may have noticed that the well-mannered and mature person has learned well the discipline of humility.

The good news is that we can implement it into our lives by the choice of our own will. And even better news is that a person with this type of humility couldn't be obscure, insignificant, irrelevant or unimportant even if they wanted to.

Wouldn't a good God give us a simple key to being happy?

I think Jesus did give us the key to being happy. It was in his answer when he was asked, "What is the greatest commandment." To paraphrase his answer, He simply said to love God and love people. He followed that by saying, if you do this you will have lived your life the way God intended a person to live.

The second part of Jesus answer became known as the "golden rule" and is still the best relationship tip ever given.

So what is this book about? This book is about the importance of nurturing our relationships and how great relationships will make us happy.

What does humility have to do with nurturing great relationships?

2

The Power of Humility

Humility is simply an attitude or approach to relationships. A good analogy might be that humility is like the Microsoft Windows program on your computer. It does not do the work, but is in the background making sure the program runs smoothly. You might also say it is like the grease that keeps an engine running without a lot of friction.

There has been a lot of misunderstanding about what humility is. In many minds the word humility is associated with a weak person with low self esteem. I contend that is a completely false view of humility.

To the contrary, humility is about emotional intelligence and the people who practice it become masters at relationships. They have a healthy self esteem and they are sought out by others for friendship and to work on teams.

What is a better definition of humility?

Since I have been speaking on the topic of the power of humility for a while, often people ask me my definition of humility. Here is my definition.

The person who approaches relationships with humility understands on a deep level who they are in relationship to God and to other people. This person is not overly impressed with himself, nor is he intimidated by others. He understands that we all stand equal before God who made us, and that our strengths and talents are mere gifts from God.

This person also has a good understanding of where he stands with God. He understands on the one hand his dependency on God, while on the other hand understands the great value he/she represents to God.

In the following chapters we will explore some ideas about how to be happier, and hopefully we will conclude that we can find more happiness by nurturing our relationships and approaching them with an attitude of humility.

We will also learn that humility is a choice. A decision to choose humility as our approach to relationships is a decision to be happier!!! The following are five areas where humility will add to our happiness.

Humility will make us happier...

1. With our relationship with God.
2. With ourselves.
3. With our inner circle of family and friends.
4. With our community.
5. With our world.

To sum up what I learned, happiness is the result of the good feelings that come from good relationships in our lives. To move towards greater happiness, we must move towards improving our relationships with God, with self, with family and friends, with our community, and with our world.

How do we maintain all these good relationships? I believe Jesus tells us the best way is found through humility.

<u>Part One</u>

How Humility will Make you Happier

with Yourself

Being Happy with Yourself is an Inside Job

The six or so inches between our ears give so many of us big problems. My goal for myself is to find a peace of mind that comes through humility. I believe that only in a peaceful mind can any happiness or joy for living exist.

A few of the humble characteristics that relate to our inner state are content, cheerful, loving, fulfilled, satisfied, at ease, matured, virtuous and true. Don't we all want these adjectives to describe us?

A friend reminded me once, that I was a human being and not a human doing. Being comfortable "in your own skin," "just being" is a confident place to be. It's a trait that requires us to understand our own worth apart from our accomplishments.

Who is really content? As a problem solver and a person of action, I seek out challenging problems to solve. I like challenges and working hard, and I can still hear my mother's words echoing, "Honey, make every move count."

5

I even take on the ultimate problem of trying to discover my purpose in life and what God wants me to do. These questions can take us out of our comfort zone for sure.

So where is the balance? What is the difference in living "in the rat race" of discontentment versus being a person who is both content and accomplished?

Do You find it Difficult to Separate Your Worth from Your Accomplishments?

I believe the real issue has to do with where we perceive our value and our identity. If we are working and striving out of a desire to be valuable, then we are in the rat race and in a bad place.

If however, we approach our work from the point of view that we "are" valuable, regardless of the outcome of our task, then we work from a purer motivation, because we see our work as a contribution to our world. This frame of reference makes a huge difference in our motivation and how we go about our lives and our tasks.

In the rat race our expectations define us and we are responsible for the outcome of our tasks. If the outcomes are not what we expected, then we are a failure. We are a failure not only to ourselves, but to all others who "buy in" to what we have sold to ourselves.

What have we bought? *That we alone are responsible for the failure to achieve the outcome we expect.* There is no place for God in this frame of reference, and this kind of thinking can be very painful. For the mathematically inclined, the formula looks like this.

Reality + Expectation = Pain + Disappointment

Or

Reality – Expectation = Contentment

The contented and accomplished person's worth is not in question when a goal is not achieved, because his worth is not rooted in the outcomes of his work. He is valuable because he exists, and he realizes it.

A task's outcome is seldom, if ever, controllable, and the outcomes are never fully known. Who can control all the intended and unintended outcomes from the actions we take? No human can, and sometimes in spite of our best efforts the ball bounces the other way.

Instead of focusing on what is uncontrollable, we must concentrate on doing our best and detach ourselves from the outcomes we can't control.

Have you Allowed your Expectations and the Expectations of Others to Give you Misery?

So what if others are expecting a certain outcome and are looking to us to make it happen? For example, our child is expecting to go to an exclusive university and they are depending on us to come through with the tuition.

These are tough situations for our egos to handle, but the person whose value is not contingent on certain outcomes has prepared himself and others for any outcome, and has the humility to accept whatever comes.

If the tuition does not manifest itself for the prestigious school, they view this not as a failure or a reduction in their value, but as a learning experience, an opportunity for improvement or a sign of divine direction.

I still struggle with linking my self-worth to my accomplishments. I sometimes fall into the trap of feeling I need to earn my way to feeling okay. Did my 401(k) go up or down today? Did I transact some business today? Did my worth diminish or grow? I feel up when it goes up and down when it goes down. When my worth goes down, I can feel worth less.

How do we get trapped into such a value system, and how do we get out?

Sometimes the most important jobs don't pay well. Being a father, husband, friend or minister to someone we care about may be number one on God's priority list for our time. Time is money, a voice nags at me. Who will I listen to? Be a father or work late? The choice can seem brutal if our values remain unsettled.

Are you Willing to Accept Life on Life's Terms?

Byron Katie wrote a wonderful book a few years ago called *Loving What Is*. In her book she tells the story of her own life. She had struggled for years with thoughts that eventually destroyed her marriage, her relationship with her children, and her career. Eventually she found herself waking up in a mental hospital.

One day she miraculously awakened on the floor of the hospital and knew she had the answers to the mental anguish she had suffered with for so long.

She learned to accept the things in her life that she could not change. Instead of struggling against reality, she embraced reality as being the way her life was supposed to be, simply because it was that way. She learned to love what is, instead of arguing with it.

She goes on to say that most of the struggle that exists in a person's life is struggling against reality. I think of my own mid-life crisis. I blush as I write my confession to using hair color. I don't think there is anything wrong with using hair color, but I used it hoping no one would notice. I was horrified if someone noticed, and they did. I was embarrassed. I even lied about it once.

I finally decided to embrace the fact that I was getting older—that my hair was turning gray—that I was becoming invisible to a whole generation of young people who cannot see gray-haired people.

Does your Struggle against Reality Give you Painful Thoughts?

It has been 10 years since I read Byron Katie's book and on many occasions I have done what she calls "The Work" on my thoughts, and with good success. I even used her technique to overcome my phobia for flying, but I still struggle with always loving what is, and truthfully I think that is normal.

I must continually find my thought patterns that make me uncomfortable in my own skin. I must examine the thoughts that get me out of a peaceful state and into one of striving, worry and regret.

It's a battle, but one that is worth fighting. It takes humility to accept reality, and humility to overcome our stubborn vision of the way things are supposed to be.

It can be terrifying to release our vision of the way things ought to be, but are not, and to embrace that our current reality is the way things should be in our life for now, simply because it is what it is. This takes a firm and courageous decision, extraordinary humility and a determined will.

"Is this the truth?" is a good question to ask ourselves. Sometimes we believe painful lies about ourselves. To believe a lie is to give power to a false reality.

If what we believe about ourselves is not the truth and we realize it, then it is easier to drop the thought and stop worrying about it. That is why I have found it productive to analyze my painful thoughts. At least I want to know if they are valid or not.

Paul the Apostle in II Cor. 10:5 talked about our need to take our thoughts captive. I like that visual, and even better I imagine torturing those painful thoughts that have been torturing me till they give me the truth. When you expose a thought for the lie that it is, then you can put it out of your mind and life forever.

However, If you determine the thought is not a lie, then you must begin the harder work of accepting a hard truth about yourself or your situation.

Are you Willing to Trust God to Work out the Bad Things that have Come into your Life?

In some areas of my life I continue to frustrate myself. I am not yet willing to do what I am trying to help others to do. It takes great trust to do it. Trust that someone (God) is there to catch you when you fall…to trust that God is here and working good things out, and that reality is one of the tools God is choosing to use on my behalf to shape me into something better.

To trust that reality is truth, at least in this moment, continues to be tough for me. If you have great trust then you don't need great courage.

I remember my niece Heidi, when she was a little girl about 2 years old, she would jump off the refrigerator into my brother's arms. She wasn't incredibly courageous, but she had lots of trust that her daddy was there to catch her. She did it many times and he was always there to catch her. One miss and it would have been another story.

Do we trust enough to believe that God is orchestrating and intervening through the turmoil and tragedies that are sometimes our life, to eventually work out good from the bad? Can we believe that God specializes in taking bad and reshaping it to bless us? It's a leap of faith to believe and it always will be.

It takes great humility to accept our reality and to trust that God is working through our circumstances to mold us into the work of art He desires, and to bring about His good purposes. To stop struggling with reality and to come to humble acceptance adds happiness to our life.

Discussion Questions:

1. According to the author, to accept "life on life's terms," is not meant to mean "giving up" or resignation. What does it mean to you?

2. How are you struggling against reality in a way that causes you pain?

3. What expectations cause you the greatest disappointment?

4. Have you allowed your expectations and the expectations of others to give you misery?

5. Are you willing to trust God to work out the bad things that have come into your life?

6. Can you think of instances in the Bible where God took bad and reshaped it to bless us? Hint: There is one big obvious one.

Chapter One

Life is Short

Teach us to number our days, that we might have a heart of wisdom.

–David the Warrior King

Have you Experienced the Illusion of Ownership?

The ideas we develop of ownership are often formed at a very early age. By the time I arrived in the world, my grandfather owned a small cattle and vegetable farm in the foothills of the Appalachians in Northwest Alabama.

He tended "our farm" from sunup till sundown, and it was a beehive of activity which all his children and grandchildren engaged in. We all pitched in for planting and harvest, and the hot job of baling and storing the hay for winter.

All us grandchildren enjoyed the land with its places to hike, explore, hunt, and fish. My grandfather "owned" the place, and he called the shots. The farm belonged to him, and as far as my short-term perspective (18 years old) was concerned, he had always owned it.

Then a strange thing happened to my perspective...my grandfather got sick, and my father bought the farm. Now my father owned the farm, and he called the shots, but it continued being a place I loved and enjoyed.

Eventually our family evolved, and my father's sons either became too busy to help with the farm or moved away to pursue their new dreams. My father sold our farm to my uncle.

Though the farm was still in the family, I noticed my access became more limited. My uncle installed a new gate with a lock. I was welcome to the key anytime I asked, but it was never quite the same or as comfortable as it had been when my grandfather or father owned it. Mentally, this all made perfect sense, but emotionally, it was an adjustment for me. There was sadness to it...a loss...like the end of an era.

Eventually it dawned on me that my grandfather had never really owned the farm, at least not in the way I had thought. Of course, technically, the county records would indicate that he had been a previous owner, but in reality, he was only the caretaker for a relatively short 30 years or so.

Before him, others occupied it and I know, from the flint arrowhead tips I found, the plot I called our farm was occupied by Native American Indians at one point.

Ownership is not only an illusion, it is also elusive. I often think of something I once treasured, like my grandfather's pocket watch, or my old baseball glove, and wonder, "What happened to that? Did I lose it...Did I give it away... Was it stolen or borrowed or did someone throw it away not knowing its value to me?"

Holding on to possessions over time is like trying to grasp sand. It eventually flows through your fingers.

I've concluded that everything is temporary here, and the sooner I realize this in the deepest of ways, the sooner I will free myself of trying to possess things. What is stylish and "in" today is soon "out of date" and disappears to make room for the new and improved.

The Power of Humility

Have you ever Felt as if Your Possessions Owned You instead of You Owning your Possessions?

A few years ago, I was spending my Saturday mowing the lawn, washing my car, dusting my furniture...you get the idea. Then the thought came to me, "Isn't this stuff supposed to be serving me?

Why am I spending my day off serving all this stuff?" With this flash of insight, I felt I understood Jesus' words when he said, "Man cannot serve two masters, for he will adore one and despise the other. Man cannot serve both God and mammon (his own possessions)" (Matt. 6:24).

That day was a turning point for me, and I began to make small changes, first in my attitudes about possessions, and later my new attitudes began to surface in how I was living my life. I had at least decided I was not going to spend as much time serving possessions.

Jesus' teachings about possessions are still radical today. He taught His disciples by asking them penetrating questions.

Jesus said, "For what shall it profit a man, if he shall gain the whole world, and lose his own soul" (Matt. 16:26)?

And who can forget the interchange to the rich man's question? (See Matt. 19:16–22.)

"Good teacher, what good deed shall I do that I might inherit eternal life" (v. 16)?

Instead of answering the man's question, Jesus perceived by the rich man's question, his flawed thinking.

Jesus said, "Why do you call me good? There is none good except God alone." (v. 17).

Obviously, the man perceived Jesus to be only a teacher, so Jesus knew that the title of good was mere flattery. The rich man had no idea that he was speaking with God Himself, yet Jesus did not correct him. Instead, Jesus attempted to shift the man's thinking and pointed him to God.

Eventually Jesus said to this rich man, "If you want to be perfect, go and sell what you own and give the money to the destitute, and you will have treasure in heaven. Then come back and follow me" (v. 21).

This must have hit below the belt to this rich young leader. Jesus' statement still opposes the values of self-made successful go-getters.

Finally, Jesus gave him something that might one day lead him to see his own inadequacy and need for someone bigger than himself.

The text says, "But when the young man heard the saying, he went away sorrowful, for he was one that had great possessions" (v. 22).

We are not given the ultimate outcome of this encounter, but knowing the amazing impact that Jesus' words have on people, I would imagine that the rich man eventually got the point by recognizing his inadequacy and determining to place himself in the hands of a gracious and merciful God.

Though I recognize my inadequacies and need for God, neither am I ready to act so radically with my finances. I choose to keep some in reserve for a rainy day. I have been saving for a day when I choose not to work or a day when I can no longer work. I hope neither of those days ever come.

Jesus said to His disciples after their encounter with the rich man, "I can guarantee this truth: It will be hard for a rich person to enter the kingdom of heaven. It is easier for a camel to go through the eye of a needle than for a rich man to enter the kingdom of God."

Do you Realize that your Stuff can be a Distraction that can Keep you from God?

Those are pretty strong words from Jesus. Most of us recognize the distraction that money and wealth can bring. Money does change most people. And when you have saved some money for retirement or made a significant amount in business or real estate, it is easy to transfer your trust to money rather than to God. And if we are tempted to say, "I am not rich," consider that one half of the world's adult population have less than $4,000 net worth and two thirds have less than $10,000.

Many of Christ's early followers did sell all and follow Him, and some thought selling everything was an essential part of following Jesus.

Have you Come to Realize that Simple is Better and Less can be More?

I am beginning to see more and more the wisdom of His words to the rich man. For starters I am on the path to simplifying my life and am assigning less and less value to material things that one day will come up missing or will be an outdated gift or possibly an unintended burden to the next generation.

I am less and less what I own, and more and more I want only to have "enough" and the ability to give to a few good works.

Our Native American ancestors seemed to get this concept of ownership better than we have. They had no concept of private ownership of land, for the land belonged to the tribe and all were entitled to its fruit. And, in the event the ground was abandoned, it was there for the use of whoever was willing to cultivate it.

Few examples better illustrate this conceptual difference of land ownership than a speech given by Chief Seattle in response to an offer made by President Franklin Pierce to buy Indian Lands. Listen to the eloquence and ancient wisdom in his words.

> *The great -- and good, I believe -- White Chief sends us word that he wants to buy land. But he will reserve us enough that we can live comfortably. This seems generous, since the red man no longer has rights he need respect....*

17

So your offer seems fair, and I think my people will accept it and go to the reservation you offer them. We will live apart, and in peace.... It matters little where we pass the rest of our days. They are not many. The Indians' night will be dark. No bright star shines on his horizons. The wind is sad. Fate hunts the red man down. Wherever he goes, he will hear the approaching steps of his destroyer, and prepare to die, like the wounded doe who hears the step of the hunter....

We will consider your offer. When we have decided, we will let you know. Should we accept, I here and now make this condition: we will never be denied to visit, at any time, the graves of our fathers and our friends.

Every part of this earth is sacred to my people. Every hillside, every valley, every clearing and wood, is holy in the memory and experience of my people. Even those unspeaking stones along the shore are loud with events and memories in the life of my people. The ground beneath your feet responds more lovingly to our steps than yours, because it is the ashes of our grandfathers. Our bare feet know the kindred touch. The earth is rich with the lives of our kin.

To face the coarse reality of the brevity of life and the temporary nature of material things is humbling. We ignore it to our own detriment.

To embrace this reality compels us to live with more awareness, more appreciation, more heart. It transforms the quality of our time and our focus to value the things here that are eternal.

Discussion Questions:

1. Have you ever had a treasure that seemed to slip through your fingers like sand?

2. What was Jesus attempting to get the rich man to see?

3. What is healthy about how the Native American viewed land ownership? What problems would their attitude prevent?

4. What problems does an emphasis on wealth and material things bring upon a man or woman?

5. How does embracing the reality that life is short help you to live with more awareness, appreciation and heart.

Chapter Two

God's Grace is for You, Too

Choose to Forgive Yourself

My dad turned 79 this year. He gets around pretty good for a fellow his age. He likes to show off by dancing a little jig around the house to prove to us that he's still got it. However, I can tell he has slowed down a bit. He tries to hide it, but sometimes I see him struggle to breathe.

Every day he has on earth is a treasure to me and I want the rest of his days to be filled with pleasant times around his house and garden.

God used a painful Easter weekend to teach me a lesson about His grace. Johnny, my one-year-old yellow Labrador retriever, and I went to spend Good Friday night with Dad and his wife Anna.

After feeding and tying Johnny to a tree on the side yard, Anna and I played a nip and tuck Scrabble game till late. Anna won as usual. On his way to bed, Dad noticed my tray filled with vowels and said, "You need to learn how to speak Hawaiian."

21

Unfortunately, words like Maui, Bikini and Oahu are the extent of my Hawaiian vocabulary. I lost big.

As usual, we rose early for a Saturday to the distinctive smells of coffee brewing and bacon frying in the skillet. Anna had prepared a great breakfast of bacon and eggs, homemade buttermilk biscuits with Muscadine jelly, thickening gravy, cantaloupe, orange juice, and hot coffee.

"Dad has it made," I thought, "but I am not sure he knows how much." Dad blessed our bounty, and I dug in until I couldn't eat another bite. "I would gain 100 pounds if I ate like this every day," I thought.

The April day was beautiful, and the morning sun had taken the chill from the air. The blooms on the trees and flowers were emerging, and the new beginnings of spring energized us with talk of projects for the summer.

Dad and I walked out on the porch to meet the day and to check on Johnny. Instead of being his usual hyperactive barking and jumping and slobbering self, he had wound himself around a tree and was still and quiet. He was knotted around a couple of saplings and crouched practically immobile.

We walked closer to see the mess he had made. His steel cord leash was as tangled as a fishing line and tightly stretched between two trees. His tugging against the leash was making his predicament worse, so I let him off the hook to untangle his leash.

Have you ever seen a young dog run after he has been tied for a while? Johnny took off as if shot from a gun. He ran so fast the grass seemed to roll up behind him. Then, all of a sudden, his rear end slid and fish tailed, and he raced back in our direction. Full speed and wide open, Johnny came straight at us. Amused at first, as he came closer I suddenly felt a tinge of danger because I realized Johnny could run full speed into Dad. At the last second he swerved to run between us and hit the cord stretched between the trees.

Dad was standing behind the cord, and it jerked to strike him across the shin. I looked up in time to see his grimace and knew he was in trouble. As we looked down, we could see the red stain growing on his pant leg.

The Power of Humility

A bit stunned by what had just happened, Dad and I walked to the porch to get a better look. (Before we pulled up his pant leg, I must remind you, the skin gets thinner as we get older, and Dad's skin is especially thin due to allergy medications taken for thirty years.)

Dad raised his pant leg. The cord had slashed into his leg to the shin bone and slid up the shin under the skin about four inches the same as you would fillet a fish. (This is killing me as I write about it.) Blood was pouring down his leg and soaking his socks. After a couple of glances, I couldn't bear the sight. By this time Anna was on the scene, and she brought a calming influence to both of us.

Anna quickly gathered some antiseptic and gauze, and she bravely cleaned up the cut the best she could. Dad said, "My skin is too thin for stitches to hold. I don't see any need to go to the hospital. We will doctor this ourselves."

My first thought was that he was probably right. I felt helpless. I could think of nothing to make the situation better. I paced around the house. I couldn't bear to look at the cut. I couldn't believe this had happened.

Thoughts began to pain me. How could I not have seen it coming? How could I have been so stupid? He might lose his leg. What if an infection sets in? This could kill him at his age. His summer is ruined. I am going to kill that dog. Why didn't I see it coming? How could I have been so stupid?

Anna bravely finished wrapping the gash, and Dad tried to make me feel better. He said, "It is not hurting too bad." I was thinking that I would have passed out by now. I prayed he wouldn't pass out.

He stood up and gingerly danced a little jig for me. I tried to act calm, but I couldn't sit still. The thoughts were stabbing me. We went for a drive in the country. We made small talk about who lives where and the way houses and roads once looked when Dad and Anna were kids. I sensed that Dad and Anna were more anxious than they were letting on. I was dying on the inside.

When we got home, I attempted to get my mind off the accident. I watched TV. It couldn't divert my attention. I got up and paced some more. I prayed silent prayers. I tried to read. Nothing helped my state of mind. I was tormented. Finally, I announced that I was going home (about an hour's drive away).

"OK, son," Dad said. "Check on me from time to time."

"Don't worry, I will," I said as I headed for home.

On the way home I re-lived the accident over and over. Each time I broke out in angry bursts.

"I can't believe I let this happen," I shouted at myself.

My resentment grew toward Johnny, the dumb, crazy, hyper dog. When I arrived home, I lay on the couch all afternoon and evening watching movies.

My mind was relieved for short periods of time. I tried to call a few local friends to unload my burden, but they were all away celebrating the Easter weekend with their families. Finally, I reached Mark Bates in Memphis, and he offered his friendship by promising his prayers.

The night was a struggle, but finally I got to sleep. The next morning guilt and fear woke me early. I called Angela Posey, a close friend who is a nurse. She made some suggestions on what I could do for Dad, and I decided the best course of action was to take him to a wound care center on Monday. This plan helped to relieve my mind, because at least now I was doing something to help.

I continued to re-live the accident, but each time the outcome was the same. Each time I exploded in anger by hitting something. Each time I growled out loud, "I can't believe I let this happen."

It was Easter morning, and I decided not to go church but instead depart to Dad and Anna's house. I was going to explain my plan and see to it that it got carried out. Along the way I continued to endure the voices in my head reminding me of my guilt. Then at once, a different wave of powerful thoughts came over me. I began to hear thoughts that I now believe were from God himself. It was as if God said,

- **This accident has happened, and I want you to believe it has happened. Yes, you could have prevented it by realizing that big dogs can be dangerous, especially around older people. This accident has happened, and I want you to accept it.**

Immediately, a well of emotion flooded over me, and I began to weep as I drifted down the long stretch of country road. Eventually, I realized I was not weeping for my dad or about this accident, but was instead weeping for myself and my own inadequacies.

I was weeping about my condition as a man. I was weeping because I am weak, mortal, short-sighted, foolish, and sinful. I wept for my unintentional and intentional sins that have hurt me and hurt others. Weeping because I want to be one kind of man but discover that I am another kind.

Again I heard thoughts coming from the same source:

I want you to forgive yourself. These things you have discovered about yourself are true. Accept them. Then forgive yourself. This is My message to you and all of mankind through the life and death and resurrection of Jesus. Trust Me. When you find yourself in the middle of messes you have made, accept them and trust Me to work through them, and I will use your mess to bless you in the end. This is My Grace. I do my best work when you call on Me in your times of trouble.

This experience on the road to Dad and Anna's, now several years past, helped me to trust in God's grace for the accident. Dad's recovery was slow and painful. There were many trips to the Helen Keller wound care center.

Most of the summer that year, Dad spent lying around with his leg elevated. We talked on the phone almost every day for two months as I received progress reports on the wound and we chatted about one thing or another.

Almost weekly, I made the drive for an overnight stay. Dad, Anna, and I watched TV together, read to each other, and discussed ways of solving the country's problems. Mostly, without saying a word, we said that we loved each other very much.

I realized this is how God can work all things together for our good. The healing process began for me when I humbled myself to the fact that I make mistakes. The work of God's grace took over from there.

Discussion Questions:

1. Do you ever feel that it is your responsibility to control everything in your environment? Do you feel that mistakes are not allowed on your watch?

2. Is it sometimes hard for you to admit that you are not all knowing and all powerful? Is this even truer when it comes to your children or others in your care?

3. What are the negative consequences to feeling you must be in control of the people and things around you?

4. Do you need to accept the reality that you have inadequacies? Is it healthy to admit that you can't fix or correct all the bad things that have happened in your past?

5. Can you admit to God that you need His help? His mercy? His Grace?

Part Two

How Humility Will Make You Happier with your Relationship with God

Suffer little children, and forbid them not, to come unto me: for of such is the kingdom of heaven.

– Matthew 19:14 AKJV

It's a Fact—People of Faith are Happier

Can I believe that I am one of billions and still be so important and valuable to God that He designed a plan to rescue me? Not just any plan either, but one that is so robust that it required Him to give His own life to save mine. It is mind-boggling to consider. And if the words of John the Apostle are true in chapter three of his short book, then the creator of the universe did all of this for the sake of love. How can I attempt to describe this strategy of God?

It is a love story so amazing, almost too amazing to be true. It is a story so mystical and fantastic that it can be hard to grasp, yet can be easily understood and accepted by a child. The story is at least 6000 years in the making and still it continues to reveal itself. To those of us who believe, it resonates in us as truth.

If you are a skeptic about the existence of God, use caution if you choose to disprove God's existence by using the Bible. Attempts to disprove God using the Bible often lead to new followers.

Who could make this stuff up...this story? I ask myself this question sometimes. It is too incredible, but this is precisely the claim of the writings of the early Christians. And these early followers of Christ were mostly Jews who were steeped in the Torah (Genesis to Deuteronomy) and the writings of the ancient prophets.

To His disciples, Jesus was the missing piece to the prophetic puzzle given to them by the prophets. He made the ancient writings of Moses (the Torah) and Isaiah and Nehemiah come to life. As they would say, the Word became flesh and He dwelt among us.

These things are what the early Apostles and Disciples believed and taught and wrote about after their encounter with the Word become flesh...the man...Jesus. So resolute was their belief in this truth *(Jesus is Truth.)* and that they saw Him after His resurrection, that most of them were executed for proclaiming it.

It takes the humility of a child to be able to accept by faith that there is a God so big that He created the universe, yet so loving that He made a way for us to live with Him forever. This faith gives us happiness because there is so much more to look forward to.

Discussion Questions:

1. In Matthew Jesus said, "Truly I say to you, except you be converted, and become as little children, you shall not enter into the kingdom of heaven" (18:3). What do you think Jesus was saying here?

2. So resolute was their belief in this truth (*Jesus is Truth.*) and that they saw him resurrected, that most of them were executed for telling it. Some say the fact that his disciples were willing to die instead of recant their stories is one of the most compelling reasons for believing in the authenticity of the resurrection. How does this influence your faith in Jesus?

3. What is the difference between believing in God and having faith in God?

4. Do you find it easy or difficult to believe that you are special and important to God?

Chapter Three

Our Happiness should Grow as we

Mature

Spiritual Maturity Begins with an Awareness of our Spiritual Need

Chandler Moseley and I were matched by Big Brothers Big Sisters (a national mentoring organization that matches mentors with children who are seeking to spend time with adult role models) when he was nine years old. One of our first conversations went like this:

"What do you want to be when you grow up?"

Without a second thought he said, "I want to be a doctor and a rock star."

"That sounds like you will be pretty busy to me," I said. "Don't you think you should only pick one?"
"No," he said, "I will be a doctor during the daytime and a rock star at night."

Isn't that just like us when we are too young to know better? The world is our oyster and we can grow up to be anything we want, or at least that is what we believe.

It is only a little later in life that we begin to see where our talents lie. We begin to recognize how strong our motivations are and we begin to develop an awareness of our strengths as well as our limitations. We all know as we grow that this awareness is essential to our maturity.

If a person turns eighteen and still thinks he is going to be a rock star, but has no musical talent or motivation to learn music, then most of us would begin to question the young person's development into maturity.

Spiritual Maturity Begins to Manifest Itself with Awareness

One of the first signs that a person is becoming spiritually aware is when he recognizes something is wrong. He becomes aware that corruption has taken hold in places within his heart, that he cannot satisfy his own spiritual needs, and that he needs something outside of himself.

It is this awareness that sends us on the great spiritual journey to seek meaning for our lives and that journey ends for many of us at the feet of God. It takes humility to become aware of our spiritual neediness, but that is a necessary beginning to finding what we need and for adding to our happiness.

Discussion Questions:

1. When did you first realize that something was wrong in your life?

2. Where were you or what were you doing when you first realized that you needed someone greater than yourself?

3. What does the author mean when he says he became aware of corruption taking hold in places within his heart?

4. What does humility have to do with realizing your spiritual need?

5. Have you found yourself at the feet of God yet?

Chapter Four

It Takes Humility to Receive an

Expensive Gift

Choose to Receive the Grace of God

How great, or powerful, or talented or intelligent must we be to receive a gift? That is a silly question isn't it, for it takes nothing to receive a gift. It can and should be humbling to receive a large and expensive gift that we don't deserve, especially when we don't have anything comparable to give back in return. That is precisely the offer Father God has made to us, and Jesus paid the price for it.

The following is my understanding of what God is offering us:

The Power of Humility

The Holy Spirit of God living in us to comfort and guide–

Security of all kinds including having our needs met—

Freedom…he whom God sets free is free indeed—

Forgiveness from God for every sin we commit—

Freedom from condemnation and judgment—

Healing to our bodies, mind and emotions—

The Heavenly Father's attention and ear—

A Family that accepts us and loves us—

Ongoing good standing with God—

Freedom from addictions to sin—

Adoption as a son or daughter—

Protection from the evil one—

Guidance in all our decisions—

Wisdom and insight—

Life in Abundance—

Inner Peace—

Eternal Life—

Joy.

Can you Accept the Offering of God?

Am I making this stuff up? Isn't this the offering of God to us? Isn't this what the Bible reveals to us? Isn't this what we long for?

Even if we don't achieve the fullness of God's offering to us here, we do have hope that there is a place the Bible calls the new heaven and the new earth that will be a dwelling place for those who love God. Eternity is a very long time.... I can't really grasp the concept of a life that doesn't end, but I accept it and believe it.

Humbly accepting the gifts of God causes us to appreciate and trust the Father's good intentions toward us, and that leads to a deeper sense of happiness.

Discussion Questions:

1. Do you find it difficult to accept the generosity of others?

2. How does it take humility to accept the generosity of others?

3. Is it difficult for you to accept the offering of God as outlined in this chapter?

4. Why does accepting the gifts of God cause us to trust the Father's good intentions toward us and lead us to a deeper sense of happiness?

Chapter Five

Accept What God has Done for Us

When we Know Who we Are, It Makes us Happier

In time, we begin to grow in the knowledge of who we are in Christ. I know I am in the process of learning who is the new and improved person I am becoming.

The best place to learn who we are in Christ is to go directly to the Scripture itself and see what it says about who we are becoming. The following is what the Word of God says about our new position in Christ:

He has delivered me from the power of darkness and brought me into His kingdom. (Col 1:13)

I am confident that God has started a work in me and will see it through. (Phil. 1:6)

I have been bought with a price and made His own. (I Cor. 6:20)

I am the salt of the earth and light in the world. (Matt. 5: 13, 14)

I have been established, anointed and sealed. (II Cor. 1: 21–22)

I may approach God with courage and confidence. (Eph. 3:12)

The Power of Humility

I have been reconciled to God through Christ. (II Cor. 5:18)

It is no longer I who lives, but Christ lives in me. (Gal. 2:20)

I have been chosen and appointed to bear fruit. (Jn. 15:16)

I will receive grace and mercy in time of need. (Heb. 4:16)

I am given strength to do all things in Christ. (Phil. 4:13)

I am free from any condemning charge. (Rom 8:33–34)

I am saved by grace through Faith in Christ. (Eph. 2:8)

All things work together for my good. (Rom. 8:28)

I am a member of Christ's body. (I Cor. 12:27)

I am washed by the blood of Christ. (Rev. 1:5)

I am a new creation in Christ. (II Cor. 5:17)

I have been baptized into Christ. (Gal 3:27)

I have been redeemed by God. (Col. 1:14)

I have been made righteous. (II Cor. 5:21)

I am no longer condemned. (Rom. 8:1, 2)

I have been justified by faith. (Rom. 5:1)

I have direct access to God. (Eph. 2:18)

The Power of Humility

I am God's workmanship. (Eph. 2:10)

I am a citizen of heaven. (Phil. 3:20)

I am accepted by God. (Eph. 1:6)

I am Christ's friend. (Jn. 15:15)

I am a child of God. (Jn. 1:12)

I am a saint. (Rom. 8:27)

Understanding and accepting these truths were my first real acts of humility in my life. Up till then, I was incapable of being humble or doing an act motivated by humility. I didn't have the mentality for humility until I discovered who I was without Christ.

It takes Humility to Trust

The next step for me as my paradigm shifted was trusting…in a Creator Father who I now believe has good intentions toward me. He is motivated by love toward me. He desires to be my Rescuer, Defender and Friend.

It takes Humility to Ask for Help

Asking Christ into my life… is my new and natural inclination. Asking Christ into my life was not to be a one-time event, but something I do on an ongoing basis and in all types of situations. I do this because I believe that the Holy Spirit of Christ dwells in me, but at the same time, my experience is that He is a gentleman who doesn't intrude until He is invited. He wants to be invited into our every day, but is content to allow us to do what we can on our own till we learn inviting Him in is better.

It takes Humility to Listen to the God who Lives Inside

The Bible clearly teaches that God has made a deposit of His Spirit to live inside of me (II Cor. 1:22). It is sort of like a down payment to remind me of who I am now. It is almost too good to be true. Honestly, it is hard for me to grasp and to believe. My mind can hardly take this in that I have the God of the Universe as my Guide who is available for me. The following is my progression as I came to this realization:

I begin to trust that His Spirit lives in me.

I begin to listen to this Spirit.

I begin to trust that some thoughts are from this Spirit.

I begin to test this Spirit by responding to His nudging.

I see results that amaze me.

The Peace I feel within feels good and I respond to it.

The Spirit gives me more direction.

I don't always respond to the Spirit.

I realize my own nature is opposed to being led by the Spirit.

I realize my own nature wants to satisfy itself above all.

I recognize my inner conflict.

Still the Spirit nudges me.

44

The Power of Humility

Some of my words I feel guided to say, and I say them.

Some decisions I feel influenced to make, and I make them.

This is an exciting and effective and fulfilling way to live.

But it is hard because of the inner conflict.

I trust even more the voice and nudge I recognize as the Spirit.

I submit to His wisdom,

To His knowledge,

To His Omniscience.

Trusting the Spirit begins to win more and more of my heart.

I still make retreats.

Living by the Spirit becomes my preferred way of life.

The Spirit Responds to Humility

I suppose this "new way" could lead to spiritual vanity and pride, but that is not the Spirit's way. That would be my old diseased way of thinking regaining its voice.

The Holy Spirit resists self-effort and operates by grace. He does not respond to vanity or arrogance or false pride. Vanity impedes the flow of the Spirit to us. The Spirit responds to humility.

It takes Humility to have Hope

What a great act of humility on the part of a man to believe in what he cannot see, and put faith in what has been done by Father God for me, for humanity, by Christ over 2000 years ago!

Yet, my faith is not completely blind as I look around me at the majesty and intricacy in His creation. It resonates within me that a Creator exists. I do not have enough faith to believe in another explanation.

There is a great hope that wells up within me for my future and the future of those I love. There is a confidence that exudes as I believe in my intrinsic value to my Creator. A passion flows out of me for humanity and the decisions we make collectively and individually.

I have a deep appreciation for the artistry and intelligence of God's creativity. There is a relief to me in knowing that I am not the result of a cosmic accident, but was intentionally formed, planned for, wanted, loved and needed to fill and perform a role I was designed for.

And finally...

There is a deep happiness that comes over me when I humble myself to believe who I have become in Christ through faith in Christ, and to accept it all because of Christ.

Discussion Questions:

1. How did it make you feel as you read about who you are or your position in Christ?

2. What do you think the author meant by the following statements? "Understanding and accepting these truths were my first real acts of humility in my life. Up till then, I was incapable of being humble or doing an act motivated by humility. I didn't have the mentality for humility until I discovered who I was without Christ."

3. Discuss the author's statement: "My experience is that The Holy Spirit is a gentleman who doesn't intrude until He is invited. He wants to be invited into our every day, but is content to allow us to do what we can on our own till we learn inviting Him in is better."

4. Respond to how the author progressed in his learning to listen and experience a relationship with the Holy Spirit.

5. Discuss the author's statement that the Spirit responds to humility.

Chapter Six

God Resists the Proud

God resists the proud, but gives grace to the humble.

– James 4:6 AKJV

A final note on our relationship with God…

The Lord Gives and the Lord Takes Away

This statement helps me to regain my perspective. The Lord blesses by giving and taking away. The Lord disciplines those He loves. I am who I am by the orchestration of God for His purposes. I am no better or worse than any other person. My journey and development are unique to me.

Humility is Understanding your Place

The Power of Humility

Where do I fit in the bigger picture? Maybe it is as simple as knowing that we are a smaller piece in the big picture. Maybe realizing there is a big picture is what we need to learn.

Humility is understanding that I am but a piece of the larger picture without diminishing my importance or significance to the whole. Happy is the one who understands who he is in Christ and that he has an important role to play.

Part Three

Happy are the Humble

How Humility will Make you Happier with Your Inner Circle

B elow are a few *humble* synonyms for us to consider as they relate to our inner circle of family and friends. Just think how we might affect the atmosphere around us if we incorporate into who we are the qualities these *humble* words represent:

> Considerate, cooperative, kind, easy going, courteous, good natured, good humored, lenient, approachable, compassionate, generous, benevolent, respectful, soft spoken, open, congenial, warm, gracious, pleasant, receptive, affectionate, companionable, sincere, sympathetic, submissive, tender, wholehearted, genuine, devoted, committed, real, abiding, concerned, faithful, loving, appreciative, attentive, thoughtful, conscientious, dependable, trustworthy, truthful, fair, impartial, reliable, loyal, wholesome, safe, mature, big hearted, forgiving, merciful, tolerant, patient…

Our Inner Circle

Who we allow into our inner circle is extremely important, and for most of us the selection is mostly predetermined. Our parents, siblings, spouse, children and childhood friends take up many of the slots in our inner circle.

Our inner circle serves many important functions in our development and maturity. They play a dual role of both sharpening and encouraging us. They are our teachers and mentors, our students, our friends and occasionally our enemies. They are the ones we give unparalleled permission to speak into our lives. They rebuke us when we need it and pick us up when we fail or become discouraged.

Sometimes weeds get into the best of gardens. Of course, a good gardener knows that to have a bountiful harvest, the weeds have to be kept in check. There are times when we too have to set boundaries with an abusive person in our inner circle. Though this is not the focus of this book, I think it bears mentioning that there are times when we must set good boundaries and practice tough love.

Chapter Seven

Give the People you Love More Chances

If you forgive others for their transgressions, your Heavenly Father will also forgive you.

– Matt. 6:14 NAS

What Are Our Relationships Worth? When I think of mercy and forgiveness they remind me of a conversation with one of my early mentors. We were talking about a betrayal I had experienced and my difficulty getting past my hurt pride.

He said, "No relationship can last for the long term without both love and forgiveness. There will be a time when you will both need forgiveness and need to give forgiveness. Once you make a decision not to forgive, the relationship is essentially over."

"It is just too hard," I said.

"Then you have made your decision. To stay in the relationship is to prolong the agony."

I have chosen this path more than once in my life. I allowed a relationship to dissolve with an old college buddy when I decided not to forgive a slight that offended me. We lost 15 years of friendship over it. I am glad to say we eventually reconciled.

What is a father or mother worth? What is a brother or sister worth? What is a close friend worth?

Is it possible to put a value on these relationships? Is it possible to put a cost on the damage done when these relationships go wrong? Do we consider the collateral damage our broken relationships cause others?

How many sons and daughters do you know that don't speak to their father or mother? How many brothers or sisters do you know that avoid family holiday celebrations? How many close friends do you know that no longer share their lives with each other?

Janet wasn't speaking to her father. It had been over a year since she talked to him when she and I had coffee and rekindled our own friendship.

"I didn't realize Joey had an alcohol problem before I met him. I mean we both drank and partied a lot before we married, but I thought after we had our baby that would all stop. Well, it didn't stop and it got worse for Joey. He couldn't keep a job, was drinking every day and he gets rude when he drinks. I just couldn't stand it anymore so I left him," Janet said.

"Are you doing okay?" I asked.

"My father and I don't speak. He essentially called me a whore."

"Why?"

"He doesn't believe in divorce."

"Oh."

"When I walked out, it was over for me. I guess he thought I had not tried hard enough to save the marriage. When he heard that I had a date with another man, he went off on me, and as I said, he called me a whore. I can't forgive him for that."

"Does he have contact with his grandson?"

"Oh yes, I still go see mother, but I make sure he is at work."

"How is your mother taking this?"

"She makes excuses for him. She says he didn't really mean it. That he is just remembering some things his mother did when his father and mother divorced."

"What do you do for the holidays?"

"They are messed up for the most part. I won't go to any of the family gatherings."

"Is that hard on your mother and brother?"

"Yeah, I guess so. My brother is mad at me because I won't 'Just get over it.' He says that I know how Dad is and that I should just get over it."

"Was your family ever close?"

"Yes, we were very close."

"So this is sort of screwing up your whole family's life?"

"I guess you could say that."

"Have you ever thought about forgiving your father?"

"He doesn't think he has done anything wrong."

"That is not what I asked you."

"I know, but it is just too hard. He should not have said that to me. I am his daughter."

"I know, but why would you want to hold on to something that is making you and your whole family miserable?"

"I don't know."

"Has your father done anything to let you know that he is sorry this has happened?"

"Yes, he bought me a very nice Christmas present."

"And what did you say to him?"

"Nothing. I ignored it. I wanted him to know that was not good enough. He can't say he is sorry for what he said."

"So you want to punish him some more?"

Janet laughed sheepishly, "I guess I do."

"Why don't you be the big person here? Why don't you let your daddy know that you love him by forgiving him? You do love him right?"

"Of course I do," Janet said with a tear in her eye. "I am just mad at him."

"Well, from here on I think it is up to you. I have one piece of advice for you. Don't wait too long."

This story has a happy ending and little did I know my advice would be prophetic. Janet reconciled with her father and they spent two wonderful years before he suddenly died of a heart attack at age 62.

Granting mercy and forgiveness to someone we love can take great humility, but for Janet, it brought her much more happiness. Because Janet forgave before it was too late, she avoided the guilt and regret that could have been a burden for the rest of her life.

Discussion Questions:

1. "No relationship can last for the long term without both love and forgiveness. There will be a time when you will both need forgiveness and need to give forgiveness. Once you make a decision not to forgive, the relationship is essentially over." Discuss.

2. What is a relationship worth?

3. What causes us not to ask for forgiveness when we know that someone is holding hurt toward us?

4. How can holding a grudge cause collateral damage to friends and family?

5. How do we overcome the grudge we hold in our heart for the one who has hurt or offended us?

6. Why does it take humility to forgive?

Chapter Eight

Be Generous with Praise

Choose to be an Encourager

Therefore encourage one another and build one another up.

– I Thess. 5:11

Bob Haggard was my high school football coach. He taught us many lessons, but the one that has stayed with me throughout my life was the power of praise.

Beginning my junior year, I was slated to take over as the new starting Quarterback. Coach knew that I was going to need a little help being the leader with the seniors on our team. We had a good team, but we could have used the added confidence and experience a senior quarterback would have given. To help make up for my deficiency he summoned me to his office for a strategy session.

"You are going to make some mistakes and your teammates are going to make mistakes. That's life. I don't want you trying to correct your teammates when they make mistakes. That is our job as coaches. I want you to always to be looking for your teammates doing something right and recognize them for doing a good job… heap praise on them."

Be a Minister of Encouragement

So, I began to make that my practice. I was surprised how many people on our team were doing things right and I developed an eye for seeing even the smallest things. The more I praised and encouraged, the more I saw our team improve. I also noticed my teammates looking to me for leadership.

Unfortunately, we didn't win a championship that year. Our team faced lots of adversity as many of our key teammates were down with injuries. As it turned out, I broke both bones in my leg during the second game of the season. Though it was a tough season for all of us, the lesson I learned about the power of praise would serve me well the next season.

The next year, our small band of brothers won 10 games, and achieved a number 3 state ranking. That is no small accomplishment in Alabama where high school football is a religion. Though we eventually lost in the playoffs, there was consolation that we lost to the ultimate state champions who were packed with Southeastern Conference (SEC) talent.

How could we achieve that? How could an average group of players, with limited talent and no Division 1 college prospects, come together to be much more than average?

There were a number of reasons, but the one that stands out to me is a culture that looked for the best in others and recognized it. This one attribute built rapport and belief in each other, and created very positive team chemistry.

At times, we all struggle with negative emotions and need to be affirmed and reminded that we are making right decisions and doing the right things. My coach helped me develop the philosophy to be stingy with criticism and generous with praise.

An encouraging word costs little, but is worth its weight in gold, and we all need it. It takes humility to focus on the successes of others, but generous praise spreads happiness and creates an atmosphere that prompts us to celebrate.

Discussion Questions:

1. Discuss Coach Haggard's instructions to his young leader to catch someone doing something right?

2. How do others respond to your encouragement?

3. The root word of encouragement is courage. Why do people need courage?

4. How does encouragement build team morale?

5. Why does it take humility to encourage others?

Chapter Nine

Allow Others the Room to Grow

Choose to be Tolerant and Patient

Love bears all things.

– I Cor. 13:7

"*He will never change.*" If you have lived long enough, you have heard someone say this. It is sometimes said before a person decides to close the door and walk away from a relationship. Though it could be true, it might signal a need for a change in perspective.

Is it possible for an irritating person to grow beyond... mature beyond the behavior that is irritating us?

Give People Time and a Chance to Grow

I try to ask myself this question before I do anything rash. If I knew this person would grow beyond this irritating behavior in three years would I continue the friendship? This question has helped adjust my perspective and helped me to focus on believing the best.

I have appreciated those who looked beyond my own immaturity to see greater potential in me. It is amazing how often it pays off to believe in others and put faith in their eventual maturity.

This topic reminds me of the story of Michael Jordan. Many say he was the greatest player to ever play basketball. Did you know that he was cut from the varsity basketball team when he was in the tenth grade?

I would hate to be known as the coach that didn't have faith to believe that Michael Jordan could be a starter on my high school basketball team! If you are wondering, the coach's name was Cliffton "Pop" Herring a name no one remembers.

On the flip side, how would you like to be the person who had the faith to see Elvis Presley as the next rock-and-roll success? That is exactly what Sam Phillips, a native of my home town of Florence, Alabama did. He took a chance on the young Presley and the rest is history.

These stories are all around us. In the neighboring town of Tuscumbia, Alabama, Annie Sullivan saw something special in the young Helen Keller and through her patience, perseverance, hard work and faith, helped Helen overcome deafness, dumbness and blindness to become the International celebrity we all know.

Allowing others the time needed to grow takes an attitude of humility. This attitude acknowledges that all people, including our self, need the time and space to grow. When we adopt this humble attitude of faith in others ability to grow, it increases the happiness of all those involved.

Discussion Questions:

1. Have you ever heard it said that a person will never change? How hopeful is this statement? Do you believe that people can change? How about mature?

2. What is the difference in changing and maturing?

3. Have you ever taken a chance on someone who needed to change? Has anyone ever taken a chance on you while you needed to change?

4. What are the rewards to sticking with someone and having faith in their ability to change?

5. Can a person's faith in another be the impetus that motivates someone to mature?

Chapter Ten

Consider the Interests of Others

Choose to be Considerate

You can get what you want in life, if you can help enough other people get what they want.

– Zig Zigler

Find a Need and Fill it. Being of service to others can often serve our own needs best.

America has the greatest economic engine known to the history of the world. It has been the envy of the world for the past 100 years. Take the bottom 170 countries out of the 190 countries in the world and the U.S. GDP or Gross Domestic Product is more than the 170 combined.

Why Has the U.S. been so Successful?

I believe it is because we are a culture that rewards the ones who serve the best.

The Power of Humility

When I was in college in the 70's I took a summer job for the Nabisco Corporation. I was hired to relieve the route salesmen during their vacations. My job was to go into the grocery stores, put the stock on the shelves and then write an order based on what was needed.

It was good summer job, and the money was decent. An interesting thing happened to me that summer while I was in Belmont, Mississippi, putting up stock in a Winn-Dixie Supermarket. A lady came onto my aisle with a pen and paper and began writing down the prices of all the items on my aisle.

Later, as I was meeting with the store manager to discuss his order, I asked him,

"Did you notice the lady in the store writing down all the prices?"

"Yes," he said. "She is in here all the time. She works for a new store in town called Wal-Mart. They tell people that they will always have the lowest prices in town."

"Are they hurting your business?"

"No," he said. 'They don't sell a wide assortment of groceries and I don't think they can last too long with their prices. They are going to price themselves right out of business."

That day Wal-Mart gained a new customer...me!!!!

Sam Walton, the founder of Wal-Mart, took a simple idea of serving the average person better than anyone else and expanded his idea with hard work to make Wal-Mart one of the greatest companies on the face of the earth. If Wal-Mart were a country, its GDP would be in the top 25. You heard it right. Wal-Mart makes more revenue than 165 countries in the world.

Sam Walton took one simple, humble idea of serving others and, because of it, he saved average people billions of dollars that they could in turn spend for education or medicines and further improve their quality of life and the lives of their families.

Looking for better ways to serve others is not only humble, but can be extremely profitable. Serving better can improve the lives of others by more efficiently meeting needs, and this adds happiness to the world.

Discussion Questions:

1. The basis of a free economy is to find a need and fill it. Can you think of individuals or companies who found a need and built a successful business around filling that need? Name and discuss.

2. Why do you think the American economic model has been so successful compared to the rest of the world?

3. The motto of The Rotary Club International is "He who serves the most, profits the best." Discuss the pros and cons of profiting from your service.

4. Is there something basically humble about finding a need and filling it? Why or why not?

Chapter Eleven

Share What You Have

Choose to be Generous

It is more blessed to give than to receive.

– Acts 20:35

Being Generous to a Child may be Your Way to Impact the World

My parents were once accused of being tired of parenting when their fifth child (me) came along. I never felt that way, but I suppose I might have been a bit of a surprise.

The tired parent accusation came from the fact that I was always at a friend's house, but it was not so much my parents trying to be rid of me as it was my constant begging to be in the middle of everything.

I was and still am a very sociable person. I always wanted to be in the middle of every group and I was usually the one dividing the sides for a game of basketball, football, baseball, Rummy or Monopoly.

This penchant for being in the middle of everything made me a beggar and a manipulator with my parents until they finally gave in and let me go visit with friends. Hillary Clinton's book, *It Takes a Village to Raise a Kid*, could have learned a lot from watching me as a kid in our village.

I was often the guest at the tables of my friends as well as accompanying them to ballgames, concerts, and movies. There were three families in particular who each fed me at least 300 meals, and, of course, as a kid, I had nothing to give in return. I learned to accept the hospitality of others, but also learned to appreciate genuine hospitality.

Today, I have numerous friends who tell me that I have a gift for hospitality. I am not sure exactly what they mean, but I appreciate the compliment.

My philosophy and motivation for being hospitable I got from these gracious benefactors of my youth. My philosophy is not to make a fuss over someone's visit. I do not try to go out of my way to impress anyone.

If I have dirty dishes...so what. I try to make people feel comfortable like these families made me feel comfortable, by being glad to see me and then treating me as if I blended in to their families.

I also try to keep little kids in my life all the time too. As a big brother volunteer–mentor, I have tried to create the atmosphere maintained by my surrogate families I grew up in. My little brothers have the run of my house and yet at the same time, boundaries are established that makes things run smooth.

The Universal Law of Reciprocity

Many years ago, I discovered a great old book called *The Supreme Philosophy of Man*. It had a section in it that discussed the principle of reciprocity. It stated that there is a mysterious universal law that exists where the universe gives back to those that are giving.

According to this law, it is impossible to "out-give" the universe. When you give to others, others will give back to you, but not necessarily the original recipients of your generosity. You could give to people who do not have the capacity to give back, and still the law works.

It reminded me of the words of Jesus when He said, *"Give and it will be given to you. A good measure, pressed down, shaken together and running over, will be poured into your lap. For with the measure you use, it will be measured to you"* (Luke 6:38 NIV).

A special thank-you goes out to Doc and Mary Bradbury, Mack and Maurine Frazier, Travis and Sue Gravitt, Merle and Bonnie Posey, and then later while in college to Morris and Patsy Pepper, Bill and Shelva Biggs, and upon my first real job in Houston, Texas, to Walter and Susan Blanchard.

I could never repay you guys for all you did for a little knotty-head kid like me, but I hope I can pass it forward to a few others before I am through.

True hospitality and generosity are given without thought of what can be received in return and add to the happiness of many.

Discussion Questions:

1. When you encounter someone with a gift for hospitality, what qualities do they possess?

2. Can you remember a person or a family being hospitable to you when you were a young person?

3. The principle of reciprocity says that when you give, others will give back to you. Have you had an experience in life that made you believe this law is true?

4. When was the last time that you thanked those who were kind and hospitable to you?

Chapter Twelve

Defer to Others

Choose to be Deferential to Each Other

My dad was a Renaissance man. He was good at a lot of things. He was a wise man too. He understood the importance of allowing me to learn some things the hard way. He would caution me, but he allowed me to try it my way.

The word *submissive* has gotten a bad rap in our culture. I disagree that submission is a dirty word, but there are enough synonyms that can help us to see a happiness principle in the concept of submission.

A few substitutes could be deferential, cooperative, considerate, courteous, gracious or even thoughtful. The real meaning is *allowing someone else to have their way* instead of imposing our way.

Submitting ourselves by allowing someone to do things their way is not a sign of weakness, powerlessness or inferiority, but instead it is an act of generosity, maturity, kindness and love toward another person.

To Give and Take is the Better Way

I think it would be unwise and downright boring to be submissive in every instance to the same person. What an uninteresting relationship that would be, and it sounds more like an enabling relationship than a mature one.

On the flip side of that, who really wants to be in a relationship where we always do things our own way? If that is the case, why do you need the other person?

To willfully and purposefully submit to another person's way of doing things is a sign of maturity, and makes way for growth in all parties. A relationship with a humbly mature person, who allows us to grow and who practices mutual submission, makes for a happier life.

Discussion Questions:

1. How can submitting to someone else's way of doing something be an act of generosity, maturity, kindness and love?

2. Have you ever been around someone who always had to do it their way? Was that good for the relationship?

3. What can we learn by doing some things another way?

4. How does it make someone feel when you do things their way from time to time?

Chapter Thirteen

Hone your God-Given Talents to Pull your Load

Choose to Contribute and be a Team Player

Champions are Not Made in the Ring...They are simply Recognized There.

My friend Rob Likens is a college football coach. One of his favorite sayings is that "everyone wants to win, but the real winners in life are those who are willing to prepare themselves to win."

I love the pageantry and the spectacle of college football. I am a University of Alabama alumnus and a Roll Tide Roll fan. Few college traditions have given us more exciting times or more wins than Alabama.

However, what happens on Saturday afternoons in Tuscaloosa or Ann Arbor, or Norman, OK are the results of a lifetime of sweat, dedication and discipline by hundreds of individual coaches and players.

I will occasionally hear the kids in my life attribute the good fortune of their friends to luck. They will say that Johnny is lucky because his dad or mom is a doctor, lawyer or businessman, and he gets to take great vacations to the mountains or to the beach.

I am always quick to point out that luck had little or nothing to do with it. It was the parents' hard work and discipline that allowed them all to go on vacation. The parents prepared themselves to make a contribution in the lives of others and have been paid well for doing it.

You Can be Successful, too

I always point out too that we can prepare ourselves to be successful too. In America, many have worked hard to see that anyone who really wants to can prepare themselves to be productive and make a positive impact on their world.

Our Choices Make All the Difference

Arnold Kemp was a veteran of the Harlem streets and spent seven years in state prison for armed robbery. As a small child, his parents had separated and his mother, a garment worker, earned hardly enough to feed the family.

At 15, he dropped out of high school, bored and seeing no future, he hustled numbers and ran dope. Later, he enlisted in the Air Force and became a communications specialist. When he got out, the personnel offices at the New York airports had nothing for him.

"My criterion for success," he recalls, "was money—money made you a big man." As a result, he and a buddy enlisted a young woman employee of the New York Telephone Company as their accomplice and pulled off a $23,000 payroll holdup at one of the company's Bronx offices.

There was no violence; they used toy pistols for the job. Six weeks later, Kemp was arrested for the first time; the girl, questioned about her sudden big-spending habits, had talked.

The only benefit of the crime, which he now calls "dumb," was that Kemp got a pretrial mental exam at Bellevue Hospital, where he became good friends with Novelist Norman Mailer, who was in for stabbing his wife, who later refused to press charges.

Given a sentence of ten to twelve years, Kemp began smuggling short-story manuscripts out of prison for Mailer's comments and corrections.

He trained himself partly by rewriting passages of Tolstoy and Dostoevsky in his own words. He also learned French and earned a high school equivalency certificate. Just before his parole, a recruiter for a New York program called "SEEK" wrote to suggest that Kemp become an undergraduate.

He got a job with an antipoverty project in Harlem and attended school at night. Soon he qualified for a $50-a-week stipend and began attending during the day, taking an accelerated 50 credits a year instead of the usual 30.

Kemp earned a bachelor's degree in three years with an average of A minus. Arnold Kemp is holder of three fellowships, and is studying at Harvard for a Ph.D. His poems have appeared in an anthology of young black poets; his first novel is in the hands of a publisher and he is well on the way to teaching English to ghetto kids.

Though our journey may start slow and have many obstacles to overcome, finding a way to be a team player and making a contribution to your family and your community are acts of humility and lead to a happier community.

Discussion Questions:

1. Champions are not made in the ring...they are simply recognized there. Discuss your observations of those who have become champions.

2. Discuss the difference in having the will to succeed versus having the will to prepare to succeed.

3. Your choices can make all the difference in your life. Discuss one decision you made that led to positive outcomes in your life.

Chapter Fourteen

Be a Person Others can Count On

Choose to be Dependable

My father never failed to have a pocket knife when I asked for it. That was something I could depend on. He found a thousand ways to use his pocket knife and couldn't understand why everyone didn't carry one.

My father was part of Tom Brokaw's greatest generation. He was a WWII veteran, a teacher, a farmer, a businessman, a husband and a father. You look up the word dependable and there should be a picture of my dad there.

When I remember his life, I can hardly recall him missing work, church or his civic club meeting. At the end of the work day he came home and began working at home, unless he was attending one of our sporting events.

He was steady and we all could depend on him to live his life in a predictable way. It is comforting to have a person like that in your life. His demeanor and leadership helped make our home a safe place.

My mother died when my dad was just 62 years old, and shortly thereafter he had his first heart attack. I guess you could say that he suffered from a broken heart. He did recover, and

81

within a couple of years he married a beautiful lady, and they had seven wonderful years together. All five of his children loved her, and she made us all feel welcome in their home.

Tragically, she died while having heart surgery of her own, and shortly thereafter, Dad had his second heart attack. Resilient as before, Dad recovered, and at the age of seventy-four married a widow who had been his secretary forty years earlier.

They had nine wonderful years of marriage before my dad finally succumbed to his third heart attack on his 84th birthday, only hours after having taught a Bible class.

Not only did my Father, Gene Mize, live in a dependable way, he also made dependable choices. Ruth Mize, my mother, Meritta Howell Mize and Anna Stockton Mize all blessed his family in many ways.

Being dependable is a character trait of the humble and makes you and those around you feel safer and happier.

Discussion Questions:

1. Who has been the most dependable person in your life? How did their dependability impact your life?

2. Why is dependability important to the success of an organization?

3. Being dependable is a quality of the humble. Discuss.

Chapter Fifteen

Be Thankful for What Others Do

for You

Choose to be Appreciative

No Man is an Island. I am not me—if you remove anyone from my past who influenced me to be who I am.

Who can take all the credit or the blame for whom we have become?

Who has any control over who their parents were? Their character? Their race? Can we control the country where we were born? Can we control what region of the country we were born? Can we control who our siblings are? Who chose their early teachers? Who carefully selected their early friends?

So much of who we are and what we have is the result of a convergence of a million variables. Who can truly say he deserves anything? Why was I not hit by that drunk driver? Why wasn't I paralyzed when I took the head-on hit in the football game? Why didn't my wife become ill? Why didn't my mother have an affair? Why didn't my brother commit suicide?

We have all experienced or had someone we know experience all the above tragedies. We all experience major setbacks and life-changing events.

Though setbacks are real and painful, and are often not preventable, we still have some choices to make. Regardless of the challenge, we all get to choose the attitude we will employ to face the challenge. We also get to choose what we will focus on.

My training and background is in business, and in business we have a general tendency to focus on what is wrong so we can fix it. This habit to look for what is wrong has served me well as a business person, but it has been detrimental in other areas of my life.

I have developed a few tools I use to help me change this negative focus when I move into other parts of life, and they have been effective when it comes to my general happiness and outlook on life.

Gratitude Journal

One good tool I have is a journal, filled with all the things I am thankful for, that I call my gratitude list. I am always adding new categories to it. I have a list of people and why I am thankful for them. I have a category for nature, the United States, my State, my community, opportunities etc. I have listed thousands of things I am thankful for.

After you have listed a few thousand things you are thankful for, you may have to get a little creative, but you soon realize there are millions of things to be thankful for.

Just taking nature alone, you can spend weeks and months learning about the ecosystems in your own back yard with all the plant, animal and insect life that exist there that bring richness to your life.

When you are adding to your gratitude list, think of characteristics that you are thankful for with each of your family members. It gets you thinking in a different way about what you love concerning your friends and family.

Make it a habit to thank others for being in your life and doing things with you. Be thankful for even the smallest things. Say thank-you to your family member who watches T.V. with you. You will probably admit that you do enjoy merely being in their presence. Watching T.V. is just something you are doing together.

Say thanks to your spouse for taking a walk with you. You might not be walking if she were not with you. Tell your spouse, your children, your parents, your coworkers, your friends, and your boss thank-you for specific things they do for you in your life.

Take a minute to think of at least some of what you are thankful for. Here are some key areas to consider: relationships with God, family and friends; health, career, material blessings, marriage, and nature.

Learn to take time to be thankful and tell others about what you are thankful for. Being thankful is a trait of a humble person and makes your life richer as you comprehend and acknowledge the value of all there is to be thankful for.

Discussion Questions:

1. How did your parents shape you into the person you are today?

2. Name some of the people besides your parents who have shaped you into the person you are today.

3. What major event in your life had a major impact on whom you have become?

The Power of Humility

4. Take a minute and write down three things in addition to family and friends that you are thankful for. Discuss.

5. Being thankful is a characteristic of a humble person? Discuss.

Chapter Sixteen

Cultivate a Sense of Wholesome

Humor

Choose to Laugh, Even at Your Own Expense

I love to laugh and I love to hear people laugh. I believe it does you good. Proverbs says laughter is like a medicine and I believe it is true.

I had a girlfriend in high school and I think the main reason I liked her is that she laughed at my stupid jokes. And what a great laugh it was. She held nothing back and she filled the room with this joyful laughter. It seemed to make everyone happy.

When I was a kid I loved to watch Red Skelton. He was a very funny physical comic and he had some wonderful standup routines with his cross-eyed seagulls "Gertrude and Heathcliffe" and the singing cabdriver, "Clem Kadiddlehopper." I still enjoy comedy and take every opportunity to have a good laugh.

It seems that some people have the gift for making people laugh. I love these masters of the one-liner who can deliver them so quick and perfectly timed.

I have been doing a little research on the clinical findings of the benefits of laughter. Here are some of the things I found.

The Benefits of Laughter:

- **Physically** – laughter boosts our immune system, lowers stress hormones, decreases pain, relaxes muscles and prevents heart disease.
- **Mentally** – laughter adds joy and zest to life, eases anxiety and fear, relieves stress, improves mood by releasing endorphins, enhances resilience, and helps shift perspective.
- **Socially** – laughter strengthens relationships, attracts others, enhances teamwork, helps diffuse conflict, promotes group bonding, increases playfulness, makes you sexier, improves spontaneity, reduces defensiveness, releases inhibitions, and encourages true feelings to emerge.

So, if you were like me when I looked at these findings, I had to ask myself…*how can I laugh more? How can I be funnier and be around more people that make me laugh?*

Here are a few of the things I came up with:

Smile more…

Not just a fake portrait smile, but a real smile…a big smile and while you are at it, make some funny faces too. Make a few Jim Carey-type goofy faces.

I started thinking about how I am around small children. When a child looks over his or her mother's shoulder, I will naturally start making funny faces at the child. In a few minutes the child is either hiding from me or s/he is laughing at me.

Why have we stopped making funny faces to adults? Don't they need to laugh too? Try it. First go to your mirror and start by practicing some funny, weird and even ugly faces. If nothing else, it will probably make you laugh, and that is worth something. After you have practiced for a while, go out and try them out on family and friends.

If that doesn't work, go to the mall. If you are not arrested, you will likely have some of the least expensive entertainment you have had in a while.

Here are some other ways to promote laughter:

- Goof off with children.
- Read the comics or buy a Reader's Digest just for the jokes.
- Listen to the Prairie Home Companion from Lake Wobegone on NPR Radio on Saturday afternoons.
- Get a joke book.
- Rent a wholesome and funny movie.
- Invite a person with a good sense of humor over for dinner.

The bottom line is that we all need to laugh more and see the humor in life. To be able to laugh at yourself is a trait of a humble person and will make you more fun and happier, too.

Discussion Questions:

1. Who are the people in your life that make you laugh the most? How do they do it?

2. Why is it easier to have fun with children? Why do we stop trying to make adults laugh?

3. The author says that laughter can improve your life physically, mentally and socially. Discuss.

4. How can we get more laughter into our lives?

Chapter Seventeen

Don't Be Distracted When it Comes to Things that are Important to Others

Choose to be Wholehearted and Attentive

Have you ever had someone look over your shoulder while you are speaking to see who else is at the party? Most of us have, and nothing can make you less popular as a party guest.

How to Win Friends and Influence People

One of the first books I read after college was Dale Carnegie's *How to Win Friends and Influence People*. It is still one of my favorite books and I still use the principles I learned in it. If you have never read it, put a bookmark here and go buy it. You will not regret it.

How has it helped me?

I became aware that most people talk about what they are most interested in, and once that topic is completed, they feel they have nothing else as interesting to talk about.

If you are friends with this person who talks only about what they know well, you hear over and over what they know till what they have to say can become quite boring. Someone probably just came to mind. We all know these people.

We even have a name for these people...and most of us have been that person at one time or another...we call them a bore.

The Dale Carnegie book taught me an important lesson. Instead of talking to people about the subject that is most important to me, talk to people instead about the subject most important to them. It is amazing how interesting you become to others when you are interested in them and what they are interested in.

Of course, as an active listener, we need to cultivate the habit of being transparent with others and allowing them to see inside ourselves when the time is appropriate. When we give people the respect of listening to them and being interested in them, they will naturally be interested in us and those things that are of special interest to us.

Obviously, all great conversation is give and take, but allowing the conversation to be about topics that others are interested in is a sign of humility. The habit of being wholehearted and attentive to others will make you more popular at any gathering and a happier person.

Discussion Questions:

1. How does it make you feel when someone is not giving you full attention but is looking over your shoulder to see who else is at the party?

2. Why would a person who is a good listener also be considered a humble person?

3. A good conversation is not always about listening. It is also sharing with others your insights and interests. How can listening earn you the right to be heard?

4. Does being heard make you happier? Why or why not?

Chapter Eighteen

Weep with Those who Weep

Choose to be Compassionate, Sympathetic and Tender

It is Human to Cry. I went over twenty years without shedding a tear. That is not completely true; there was one time I will tell you about later. I know there are others reading this now that may have had a similar experience of your tears drying up.

When I was just getting my feet on the ground in my first job after college, a surgeon walked into my mother's hospital room, where my father, three brothers, my sister and I were waiting on the outcome of her surgery.

The doctor had a sheepish look on his face as he said, "I am sorry, but we did not try to remove any of the cancer. It was too extensive and we simply closed her back up. I am sorry."

I began to do what was natural for me in that moment. I began to weep and wail at the thought of losing my mother.

My father, the old WWII vet, in his best commanding voice, ordered me to "Stop it, Clay."

I did stop it and I did not shed another tear through the following weeks of her sickness and her eventual death. I did not

95

cry again until my father's death 22 years later, when I was finally free to cry.

I loved my father and he certainly was not a bad man, but he taught me by his command that it was not okay to cry no matter how dire the circumstance. Fortunately for me in those 22 tearless years, I learned how not crying is unnatural and un-human. Nothing is more human than crying.

From time to time, I will have people, who tear up in my presence, apologize to me. I immediately say, "Please do not stop crying; I love to see people cry."

I am sensitive to a person's pain, but I know how important it is to cry and to feel deep feelings rather than suppress them and disallow them. So, please go ahead and cry. It is good for you. It is good for the soul. It is part of being human. Cry your heart out. And when you are through crying, know that you have acted naturally and that it was good for you.

Over 95 verses in the Bible speak of people weeping. The mighty men of David wept. Wise King Solomon said there is a time for weeping, and the shortest verse in the Bible simply says, "Jesus wept" (John 11:35 NASB).

One of my best friends over the past 20 years has had a job that has moved him all over the U.S. We have faithfully kept up with each other, getting together when we can and usually managing to see each other once a year. I tell you this because the defining moment in our friendship came the night we gave my friends Rob and Soni Likens a going-away party.

At the close of the party, each of us gave them an affirmation of our friendship, and when it came my time, I wept as I spoke...my first tears since the death of my mother. Even I did not realize how deeply I felt and how important our friendship was to me.

Weep with those who weep (Romans 12:15b NASB). Show the depths of your heart. Weeping signifies a humble heart, and leads to deeper happiness.

Discussion Questions:

1. Why do you think it is so hard for some people to cry?

2. Do you think God created us with emotions on purpose? Why or why not?

3. Can you remember the last time you cried? Was it good for you to cry?

4. How do you feel when you see others cry?

Chapter Nineteen

Say... I Love You. Good Job. I Think You are Smart.

Choose to Affirm One Another

Accept one another, then, just as Christ accepted you, in order to bring praise to God.

−Rom.15:7

I am a member of a small group who meets weekly in each other's homes for friendship and fellowship. When we originally formed our group, we started out our first few meetings with an icebreaker. The purpose of the icebreaker was not only to introduce, but to affirm, each other.

We started by picking one person, and everyone in the group was asked to say one positive thing they had noticed about the person in the short time we had been together. It was amazing how much was perceived among people who had just met, and how this short and affirming time together created a loving, warm and inviting spirit and began knitting this group of people together.

A few years ago, Bonnie Posey, a surrogate mother in my youth and a dear friend now, invited me to join a mission trip to

The Power of Humility

Oho, New Mexico. She and her husband Merle were leading a group of people for the purpose of sharing God's love by inoculating the local sheep population for the Navajo Indian Nation. I accepted the invitation.

Our first day consisted of chasing, cornering and horse-collaring about 800 sheep. Our group of 15 sheep-herding and inoculating novices was taking a much-needed break before we headed to the next ranch. I had to do a double-take when I saw one local Navajo man dressed like a cowboy. Do you see the irony in that, as I did?

Anyway, he brought out a sawhorse and on one end he had built a wooden cow's head with horns. The purpose of this unusual-looking cow/horse was for lasso practice. We all took our turn swirling the lasso around our head attempting to perfectly time the release so that the loop would fall down over the cow's head. It is harder than you might think, but with half a dozen or so tries, I finally hit the target as most everyone else did.

One of our friends had her two daughters, Amy and Jill ages 12 and 15, who were along that day to observe and help where they could. Amy had watched patiently as the adults roped the wooden animal, and then, after she had waited as long as she could stand it, she popped up and said, "Let me try, please."

With a bandana around her neck and pigtails flowing out of a straw cowboy hat, Amy began her attempt. Just getting the rope to swirl was a challenge, but once she got the hang of that she began feebly throwing the rope at the wooden calf. Time and again the feeble throw fell far short. It was obvious to all of us that she was frustrated, and I felt it was only a matter of time till she gave up her attempts.

Then her older sister Jill, who too saw the struggle, said the most transformational thing I have ever witnessed. She said to her sister, "Come on, Amy, I believe in you."

Amy's entire demeanor changed and her energy level picked up and she began with a renewed effort to rope the calf. Another 6 or 7 throws and finally Amy roped the calf. Amy squealed with excitement as did her sister Jill and they hopped around in sisterly glee.

100

I learned a lesson that day. I learned the power of "I believe in you." It takes a humble attitude to affirm others, and it adds to everyone's happiness.

Discussion Questions:

1. Give some examples of affirming words to others.

2. When was the last time that you said something to affirm someone and you noticed that your words had an impact?

3. Why do you think Amy's words "I believe in you" made such a difference? What happens when we know people believe in us?

4. Who has been the person in your life to affirm you and let you know they believe in you?

5. Think of two people whom you would like to affirm, and resolve to do it.

Chapter Twenty

Hold Hands, Give Pats on the Back, Scratch, Tickle, Hug and Kiss

Choose to Touch with Affection

Peter said to him, "You shall never wash my feet." Jesus answered him, "If I do not wash you, you have no share with me." Simon Peter said to him, "Lord, not my feet only but also my hands and my head!"

John 13:8–9

Most of us don't practice the ancient custom of foot washing these days, but it obviously meant something to Jesus and to the culture of the Hebrews around the first century. It was somewhere around the year 30 A.D. when Jesus sat in an upper room with His best friends. (See John 13.)

He wanted to teach them one more important lesson before He would teach them the granddaddy of all lessons on the cross. For His last act with His disciples, He chose to wash their feet. This was the last act that He would leave for them to remember. It was an act that was the defining example of His ministry to us and an example to all who would endeavor to follow in His footsteps.

Before dinner He took a bowl and towel and began to wash His disciples' feet, one disciple at a time. It was customary for the youngest child in a household to wash the feet of guests in the household. The duty fell to the least in status, but today Jesus took up the bowl and towel and made His way around the table to wash their feet.

Peter balked at such a breech in protocol and instead reminded Jesus that He was their leader. The disciples expected Jesus to ascend to the Kingship of the Jews, and no doubt the subject had been discussed privately among them for months.

Jesus rebuffed Peter and said, "If you will not allow me to wash your feet, then you can have no part of me" (John 13:8).

Then Peter said in essence, "If you put it that way then wash me from head to toe."

We don't know if Peter's motivation was affection and love for Jesus or his desire to be a part of the new administration he was expecting. Whatever his motivation, he relented and allowed Jesus to affectionately wash his feet.

The Dream

Several years ago I had a dream that truly puzzled me. I dreamed that I was washing the feet of a black minister and as I looked up, I saw a sanctuary filled with faces of color. The place was packed. Then I woke up.

The next week at church I pulled aside a couple of black friends from my church and told them about the dream. They suggested we pray about the dream and see what God might do. I filed it away as simply an interesting dream.

A couple years later, I met a man we called Pastor Sawyer. I had met Pastor Sawyer during my involvement with a national Christian men's movement called Promise Keepers. Pastor Sawyer was a powerful man who reminded me of my high school football coach.

The Power of Humility

I remember him telling me about how he ran from the call of God on his life to become a minister, and how the Lord finally wore him down till he acquiesced. He invited me to visit his church some day for worship services. His church was Mt. Moriah Primitive Baptist Church, and without any intention of following through, I said I might surprise him someday.

Many months went by and I needed a change from my church-going routine, so that morning I called Katie and asked her if she would like to join me at Pastor Sawyer's church for the Sunday service. She said she would love to, and off we went.

It was a larger church than I expected with a full house of approximately 400 members. We were the only Caucasians in the house! The sermon was powerful, and Pastor Sawyer was an animated preacher as he paced back and forth around the platform with his red and white robe flowing behind him.

Somewhere during his sermon, he mentioned that the next Sunday was going to be their annual foot-washing service, and everyone was expected to be there.

When I heard the announcement, my heart began to race as I thought about my dream. Could it be that God truly wanted this nighttime dream to be realized? Was it possible?

My mind raced, wondering if this was God's fulfillment to my dream, and I whispered a little prayer that the Lord would let me know if this was His doing. I said, "If this is You, give me an opportunity to say something to this church," thinking that it would not happen. After all, I am a guest at a new church. Why would I be asked to speak?

As he was wrapping up his sermon, Pastor Sawyer looked out over his audience and said, "Is there anyone here today that has anything to say?"

Well, I thought my heart was going to beat out of its chest cavity. No one spoke. It was quiet as a mouse in the sanctuary and then he looked straight at me and said, "Clay is there anything that you would like to say?"

I guess the Lord could not have made it any more plain than that, and I slowly came to my feet.

"Yes, Pastor Sawyer there is something I would like to say. A few years ago I had a dream that one day I would be in a black church and I would be on the stage with a black pastor washing his feet. I never expected it to happen, but I am here and it is too big a coincidence that next week is your foot-washing service. Can I come here next week and wash your feet?"

He looked back at me nearly as shocked as I was and said, "Far be it for me to stand in the way of the Lord. I will see you here next week."

The next week came, and I attended the Mount Moriah Primitive Baptist Church in Florence, Alabama. Pastor Sawyer called me up to the platform. He asked me to take a seat and he began to wash my feet.

When he finished, we traded places. I then knelt with my towel over a bowl and poured water from a pitcher. I slipped off Pastor Sawyer's shoes and socks and began to wash his feet, and as I did I looked up long enough to see the scene of the whole church as they looked on. This was the vision I had in my dream!

Physical affection is powerful whether it is patting a young boy on the back for a job well done, hugging a grandchild just because you love them, kissing a cheek to let someone know you notice them, or scratching and tickling someone you love as you watch a movie together.

It takes humility to wash another's feet. It also takes humility to break through a cultural norm and touch another with affection. Showing affection in almost all situations makes for a happier place to live.

Discussion Questions:

1. Why do you think Jesus rebuked Peter when Peter said he would not allow Jesus to wash his feet?

2. What do you think the people in Pastor Sawyer's church were thinking as they watched the author and Pastor Sawyer wash one another's feet?

3. Why do you think touching someone in an appropriate way can be so powerful?

4. Touch is one of the love languages mentioned in Gary Chapman's book, *The Five Love Languages*. Why do you think *touch* made the list?

Chapter Twenty-One

Be Willing...

To Do New Things, Go to New Places, Meet New People on Others' Schedules, Even When You are Not yet Interested

Choose to be Companionable

For the whole law is fulfilled in one word: "You shall love your neighbor as yourself."

– Gal. 5:14

*M*elinda visited our fellowship group. She later confided that she did not really like it.

"The group is a little too diverse and not quite on my wavelength," she said to me after a meeting. "For some reason

I'm strangely motivated to come back and to continue coming back."

It was in our group she met her husband within a few short months.

"I am so happy I resisted my initial feelings that our group was not for me," she said.

I have a good friend who I think misses a lot of the richness of life. He essentially refuses to do anything that is not his idea. He does have many great ideas. He has so many great ideas, I think he feels like he is wasting time with the ideas of others.

I have a cousin who is just the opposite. Her dad used to say, *"Sarah could care less where it is you are going; she just knows that she wants to go."*

She reminds me of my old Labrador retriever, Johnny. Every time I opened the door to my truck, she jumped in to go.

I think that I want to be somewhere in the middle of those two extremes.

I loved the movie, *The Bucket List.* In the event you did not see it, the movie was about two men, both diagnosed with a terminal illness, who met while sharing a hospital room. Both men had doubts about how well they had lived their lives.

Edward Cole was a rich businessman who had for his efforts a lot of money and broken relationships. He was angry, yet realized too late that he had built his life on the wrong foundation. Carter Chambers, on the other hand, was a family man who felt that he had lived life too safe and close to home.

The two men contrived the idea of a bucket list as they contemplated the rest of their lives. It was all the things they wanted to do before they "kicked the bucket." They decided to do it together and see the world while they had time.

There were three great exchanges worth noting.

1. The first is a letter written to Edward Cole by Carter Chambers in response to a conflict and argument while on their quest, that resulted in their going their separate ways.

Dear Edward,

I've gone back and forth the last few days trying to decide whether or not I should even write this. In the end, I realized I would regret it if I didn't, so here it goes. I know the last time we saw each other, we weren't exactly hitting the sweetest notes—certainly wasn't the way I wanted the trip to end. I suppose I'm responsible, and for that, I'm sorry. But in all honestly, if I had the chance, I'd do it again. Virginia said I left a stranger and came back a husband; I owe that to you. There's no way I can repay you for all you've done for me, so rather than try, I'm just going to ask you to do something else for me—find the joy in your life. You once said you're not everyone. Well, that's true—you're certainly not everyone, but everyone is everyone. My pastor always says our lives are streams flowing into the same river towards whatever heaven lies in the mist beyond the falls. Find the joy in your life, Edward, my dear friend; close your eyes and let the waters take you home.

2. *Then a short time later Carter died and Edward Cole gave the eulogy at his friend's funeral:*

Good afternoon, my name is Edward Cole. I don't know what most people say at these occasions because in all honesty, I've tried to avoid them. The simplest thing is, I loved him and I miss him. Carter and I saw the world together, which is amazing when you think that only three months ago we were complete strangers. I hope that it doesn't sound selfish of me, but the last months of his life were the best months of mine. He saved my life, and he knew it before I did. I'm deeply proud that this man found it worth his while to know me.

The Power of Humility

In the end, I think it's safe to say that we brought some joy to one another's lives, so one day, when I go to some final resting place, if I happen to wake up next to a certain wall with a gate, I hope that Carter's there to vouch for me and show me the ropes on the other side.

3. In the movie, we know that Edward Cole reconciled with his daughter, and as only movies can do, at Edward Cole's funeral, Carter Chambers eulogizes from the grave regarding his friend.

Edward Perryman Cole died in May. It was a Sunday in the afternoon and there wasn't a cloud in the sky. He was 81 years old. Even now, I can't claim to understand the measure of a life, but I can tell you this: I know that when he died, his eyes were closed and his heart was open, and I'm pretty sure he was happy with his final resting place because he was buried on the mountain, and that was against the law.

The Bucket List inspired me to get out my old bucket list—I already had a list like this, but did not know what to call it. I have recently added a few new things to the list. I also asked someone to share some of my bucket-list experiences and I promised to share some of hers, too.

Since then, we visited the Rocky Mountains for her first ski trip (her list). We went to the Kentucky Derby (my list), and to see the Broadway play *Wicked* (hers), eat dinner in a Pakistani restaurant (hers), bought a rappelling harness to go on a rock-climbing trip (mine), and bought two bicycles so we could explore my neighborhood (mine).

It takes an attitude of humility to look after the interests of others and be a good companion. It also adds a great deal to your own happiness.

Discussion Questions:

1. What is the drawback of always doing what you want to do, when you want to do it?

2. Are you willing to try some things you don't like just because your partner or friend wants to do it?

3. What are some benefits of learning to like something new?

4. What is humble about being willing to do what you don't like just because your partner or friend wants to do it?

Chapter Twenty-Two

Don't be Negative in your Attitudes

or your Speech

Choose to be Positive and Pleasant

Finally, brothers, whatever is true, whatever is honorable, whatever is just, whatever is pure, whatever is lovely, whatever is commendable, if there is any excellence, if there is anything worthy of praise, think about these things.

– Phil. 4:8 ESV

No one wants to listen to me when I am grouchy. Neither do they respond to me the way I would like. Usually, they use my grouchy attitude as an opportunity to get away from me.

God Does Not Like a Grouch

The Power of Humility

There is something unique about a complainer. He takes a bad situation and makes it worse by adding a bad attitude. The Bible seems to tell us that God is sympathetic to a bad situation, but if we meet it with a sour and complaining attitude, He does not come so quickly to our rescue. Instead he allows our situation to worsen till our situation breaks us or softens us.

That is exactly what happened to the children of Israel after they crossed the Red Sea on dry land and went into the wilderness. I used to think they were lost in the wilderness, because the Bible says they wandered in the wilderness.

Well the truth is they were never lost, they just did not know how to get out of their wilderness. They entertained the idea of going back to Egypt to be slaves again, because they did not want to face their fears and go up against the giant Canaanite people.

Faced with slavery on the one hand and fear on the other, they chose to remain in their discontented wilderness. It was not good, but it was not as bad as Egypt and it was safer than facing the giants of Canaan, or so they thought.

God had told them He would go before them and ensure their victory. So instead of being courageous and full of faith in the future, they gave in to their fear, became grouchy and complained about their circumstances.

God said, paraphrasing, "Okay, have it your way. I will allow you to stay in the wilderness till all of you complainers die off. Then we will go in and take Canaan." And that is exactly what happened.

All the adults of Israel which were estimated at 1.5 million people, except for two, Joshua and Caleb, died in the wilderness. (If you get a chance, read the stories about Joshua and Caleb in the book of Numbers and the Book of Joshua in the Bible.)

Is the complainer in you keeping you from taking the land that lies before you? Are your fears standing in your way? Maybe you have forgotten the dream God put in your heart. Maybe you have been fearful and faithless so long, you have settled for the crumbs of life.

Is your life beyond redemption?

Are your dreams too far gone?

Are the giants in the land still too big for you?

Or are you ready to move ahead or die trying?

If you are ready to move ahead or die trying, then a good place to start is by keeping a close watch on your tongue and the words that you speak. Make a decision to stop complaining.

Make a decision to speak words of faith and hope for the future. Make a decision to believe that God will help you if you choose to have faith in Him and His ability to help you.

Life and Death are in the Power of the Tongue

The Proverb says, "Death and life are in the power of the tongue, and they who indulge in it shall eat the fruit of it [for death or life]" (Prov. 18:21).

Life and death are in the power of our tongue? That is a lot of power. That makes the choice of our words monumental. Do we bring life to the things we talk about? Do we bring death to them? It is sobering to think something more lethal than a gun and more healing than medicine lives in my mouth.

When we speak pessimistically about our jobs, the future of America, our leaders, the economy, or our finances, we are speaking death to them. To speak death brings fear, and fear causes us to retreat, hunker down and go into our caves.

When we speak optimistically, our words bring life to our companies, our country, our leaders, the economy and our finances, and give us confidence to act. Our positive words encourage us to be engaged and to take advantage of opportunities as they present themselves.

116

There are plenty of reasons to believe in an optimistic future if we want to. As a Christian who loves God, I think the best reason we have to be optimistic is because God promises us that all things will work together for our good (Romans 8:28).

At least as far as this side of heaven is concerned, what better promise can we have than that? Just as God promised Israel that He would go before them to defeat their enemies, we are assured that God himself is on our side working things out.

It takes a humble person to keep watch over his words and attitudes and keep them positive and pleasant and faith-filled. It also adds to a person's happiness and all those around him.

Discussion Questions:

1. When we complain, what does it say about our faith?

2. Are we attracted to people when they are complaining? Why or why not?

3. Life and death are in the power of the tongue. Discuss.

4. Give an example of how someone used words to change the atmosphere of a situation?

5. It is easy to speak pessimistically. What are some ways we can resolve to speak optimistically about the situations we find in our lives?

Chapter Twenty-Three

Don't Be Too Busy, Too Smart or Too Important

Choose to be Approachable

In your relationships with one another, have the same mindset as Christ Jesus: Who being in very nature God, did not consider equality with God something to be used to his own advantage; rather, he made himself nothing by taking the very nature of a servant, being made in human likeness.

– Phil. 2:5–7 NIV

At one time or another, most of us have regrets for roads not taken in life. Mine was when I chose business over teaching and coaching. Business was the practical choice I thought when I entered college. Business had more earning potential and stability, and coaches are often on the move from town to town.

During the halftime of my life, I again found myself contemplating my career future. Larger insurance companies gobbled up the two mid-size insurance companies I built my career around as an independent insurance marketer. Key individuals, with whom I had built strategic relationships, were transferred or downsized, and I was effectively out of business.

In a strange way, being forced to start over made me happy. It had been a while since I had wanted to jump out of bed to get to work. I was burned out, but had not admitted it. It became clearer the night I watched the movie *Breakable* with Bruce Willis and Samuel Jackson.

The movie begins with a terrible train crash and David Dunn, played by Bruce Willis, as the sole survivor. David is a down-and-out security guard at a rugby stadium, and his marriage is on the rocks. When he attends the funeral of the victims of the crash, he finds a letter on his windshield asking, "How many days of your life have you been sick?"

David begins to think about it and realizes that the answer is "none," and contacts the sender of the letter. Elijah Price is the owner of a comic book store. Elijah has a serious illness. His bones are very fragile and are always breaking.

The reason Elijah approached David with this question is that he wants to prove a theory he has formulated. His theory is that if there is someone like himself on one end of the bell curve, a highly "breakable" man, there must be an opposite at the other end of the curve, the "unbreakable" superhero.

David rejects the idea and sees Elijah as some sort of con artist trying to scam him, but just prior to rejecting Elijah's theory, David delivers a very cutting line in the movie.

He said, "Did you know that this morning was the first morning I can remember, that I didn't open my eyes and feel that sadness—do you know what I'm talking about? That little bit of sadness? I thought the person that wrote that note had an answer for me—for why I survived that train wreck; for why my life feels so out of balance."

Later in the movie Elijah says to David, "And that little bit of sadness in the mornings you spoke of? I think I know what that is. Perhaps, you're not DOING what you are SUPPOSED to be doing."

The Power of Humility

As the movie progresses, David begins, slowly at first, to see himself differently, and begins to suspect he does in fact have unusual gifts. That he has skills and training that help him to better protect others. In turn, his self-respect begins to return, and his relationship with his wife and son improves. He stops blaming himself and his wife, and stops focusing on his regrets. His sense of purpose for living begins to be restored.

Because Elijah recognizes David's potential, David begins to test his own limits. David opens his eyes to the truth that he is special and that he does have super powers.

David's belief in Elijah's theory continues to grow. His vigor for his work returns. He recognizes that he is especially gifted and equipped as a security officer.

He realizes his job is not just a job but is a true calling. He begins to see the necessity of his role in the world. Now when he goes to work, he listens to his instincts that will help him save the innocent and unsuspecting. In case you haven't seen the movie, I won't ruin the ending for you.

I bring all this up because it relates to my own story, my own struggle to find my superhero qualities or at least find the gifts that best contribute to other people. What are my God-given gifts? How can my gifts give me a sense of purpose and joy that come from doing what I am supposed to be doing?

I discussed this subject over coffee with the usual suspects, Steve and Larry. I discussed a huge career leap. After my own career train wreck, I decided it was time to visit the scene of my regrets. Therefore, I volunteered to coach middle school football.

"I loved my first year as a volunteer football coach. There is just something special about the way some of the kids look at you. Like they are looking for a father and they see one in you. It is very gratifying," I said to Larry and Steve.

"It would be tough to start a coaching career at your age," Steve said.

"Yeah, I know. I would need something really big to kick start me. Something big to give me a name and instant credibility," I said.

"How could you get that?" Larry asked.

"Wouldn't it be awesome to work for Mark Richt at The University of Georgia?" I asked. "Just from what I know of his story, he is a first-class person as well as a coach, and he doesn't suffer from a gigantic ego like some coaches you hear about."

My buddies sort of rolled their eyes at my suggestion, saying to me that I needed to come back to the real world. I took their body language as a challenge and said that I was going to go visit Mark Richt and ask him if I could be a volunteer on his staff while I went back to school to get my teaching certificate. It would be a bold move, and if by some slim chance it worked out, it would provide the impetus for making such a drastic life change.

"I figure that if I am able to work for Coach Richt's staff for a couple of years, I wouldn't have any trouble getting a head-coaching job at some small or mid-size high school in the south. Maybe some school system looking for maturity and a good story."

This was December and Georgia had just finished their final game of the regular season and was preparing for a New Year's Day bowl.

"I am going see Mark Richt," I said with conviction.

"Where are you going to see him?" Steve said.

"I am going to Athens, Georgia."

"Yeah, send us a post card," Larry said.

"Seriously, I am going," I said.

"Well, you better do it before you think about it too long,"
Steve said.

*I was packed and ready, and by two o'clock, I was on the road
to Athens, Georgia. Six hours later, I checked into an on-campus
hotel and went looking for the athletic complex.*
*I wanted to be sure I was ready to go the first thing Friday
morning. I did not sleep too well, but I awoke early, put on a suit
and tie and was at Coach Richt's office by 8:00. I managed to get
past the receptionist by telling her I had personal business with
coach Richt, and she let me in to see his personal secretary.*

*"Hello, my name is Clay Mize and I was wondering if I could
see Coach Richt this morning?
"*

"Do you have an appointment?"

"No, I don't."

"Can I ask what this is about?"

"Well, it is personal."

*"Coach Richt is in town today, but he is very busy. He has a
bowl committee meeting and recruits coming in today."*

*"I know I don't have an appointment, but could you ask him
if he will see me?"*

*"I will call him on his cell and tell him you are here to see
him."*

"Thank you."

The Power of Humility

"Well," the secretary said, surprised, coming back to the waiting room. "He is on his way into the office and he said that he will meet with you."

"That's great, thank you."

When Coach Richt arrived, he invited me in to his private office. The walls in his office were appointed with the rich tradition of Georgia football and he directed me to sit at a small conference table where I imagined many future NFL players sat with their parents as he laid out how Georgia would be a great new home for these anxious young men.

We sat and talked liked old friends, and at no time did I feel like he was in a hurry or that I was an imposition to him. After hearing my proposal, he let me down easy while at the same time affirming me in my quest to find my higher calling.

He seemed to appreciate that I was looking for a new way to help and impact young people for good. He also made some suggestions in the event I continued pursuing a coaching career. I left the meeting feeling as if I had been in the presence of a great man.

I am still looking for ways to use my God-given gifts. I am still evolving. I coached another two years of middle school football, I completed a novel that was good in places, I redesigned my business plan, I became certified as a business coach, and I am writing this book—all efforts to evolve into a higher calling.

Never think yourself too important, or too busy, to be approachable by friends, family, acquaintances and even strangers. You never know where people are on their journey, and that you might have exactly what they need to help them move to their next level of growth and development.

My mother was always courteous to strangers, and once she let me in on her motivation. She said, *"You never know when you might be entertaining Angels unaware."*

While I may be tempted to give off an air of importance when things are going well, I realize that what I am actually doing is isolating myself by making myself less approachable. It takes a humble attitude to be approachable, but it is a building block to more and better relationships and to a happier life.

Discussion Questions:

1. Do you know someone who has an important position, but remains approachable? How does that make you feel?

2. Have you ever had a friend who rose to a high position and you felt as if you lost access to him/her? How did that make you feel?

3. "You never know where people are on their journey, and that you might have exactly what they need to help them move to their next level of growth and development." Discuss the author's statement.

Chapter Twenty-Four

Ask for Help When You Need It

Realize You Have Unmet Needs

I will lift up my eyes to the hills. From where does my help come? My help comes from the Lord, who made heaven and earth.

— Psa. 121:1–2

*W*e ask for Sandy when my pastor Mark Maybrey and I meet for lunch at "The Garden Gate," our favorite country-style restaurant. She sang as she whizzed by our table dropping off water and silverware.

"Sandy, what are you so happy about?" I said.

"I just am," she said. "I am happy in my heart."

"I think to analyze happy is to ruin it," Mark whispered as Sandy rounded the corner.

"Yeah, my mother told me once that I think too much. She said I would be happier if I didn't analyze so much."

A few minutes later I heard Sandy laughing as she put ice into a glass. I called her over.

"Sandy, why are you happy in your heart?" I asked.

"Because God loves me and you love me, too. And I want to be happy. There are some days I don't feel like being happy, but generally I want to be happy, so I am," she said as she hurried to the next table.

"See I told you. You are either happy or you are not. To think about it is to ruin it," Mark said.

"Yeah, but did you hear what she said? She said she was happy because God loves her and I love her, too. Isn't that kind of what Jesus said, when He was asked, 'What is the great commandment?' He said the greatest commandments are to love God with all your heart, soul and strength and to love your neighbor as you love yourself.

Sandy has inverted it and turned the positive power of it onto herself. I can see how living with the realization that God and our neighbors love us could impact our sense of well being and make us feel happier."

"That is an interesting thought, but there you go analyzing happiness again. I still think you have it or you don't."

"I agree, but there is a reason a person is happy whether they realize it or not. Did you notice how she ended her last sentence? She said, 'I want to be happy, so I am.' Isn't that what God called Himself...I AM? Don't you think there is some happiness in knowing that you are...that you exist and that your existence counts for something?"

Mark nodded.

We all have needs. When our needs are met, it produces a sense of satisfaction that increases our joy for living. We all need to be loved, even those of us who push others away, because "feelings" make us uncomfortable, need to be loved.

Needing love is a part of being human. It is how God made us. Don't be afraid to reach out to others to have your needs met. It is humbling to admit you have needs you can't fulfill yourself, even the need to be loved, but it is essential to happiness.

Discussion Questions:

1. Sandy said she was happy because God loved her and so did I. Why do you think she said that made her happy?

2. Do you think wanting to be happy has an effect on happiness? Discuss.

3. It is sometimes hard for us to admit or even realize we have unmet needs. Discuss.

4. Do you feel like you have a few people in your life whom you can reach out to when you need love or friendship? Discuss.

Chapter Twenty-Five

A Soft Answer Turns Away Wrath

Choose to be Soft-Spoken

It's a given that if you live in close proximity to another person for very long, there will come a time when you will get on their nerves. To think otherwise is unrealistic.

My dad could be a barker. He learned his way of getting things done from his WWII Drill Sergeant. I hated it, but tolerated it because he was my father, but I can't take that tone from anyone else. The tone I call "the voice," can send me over the edge.

Someone used "the voice" on me the other day. I own an old building in a historical part of town. It is quaint and nostalgic, but it is also prone to problems that come with being 150 years old.

My building butts right against my neighbor's old but newly purchased building, and he was endeavoring to fix a persistent drainage problem in the basement of his building. There had been a small puddle of water in a section of this basement for years.

He diagnosed his problem as being a slow-leaking water pipe that was coming from my building. It was at 6:00 P.M. on a Saturday when he called to tell me about his, "now my," problem.

The Power of Humility

I was looking forward to my own "date night," and I told him I would look into it on Monday. It was then he demanded in "the voice" that I fix the problem immediately.

A little stunned, as I always am, by "the voice," I became furious as he continued to speak to me like he was the drill sergeant father and I the stupid son. When the call finally ended, I was mostly furious for allowing him to talk to me the way he had.

The more I thought about how he talked to me, the madder I got. I haven't been in a fist fight since I was in the sixth grade, but I found myself day-dreaming about punching this man in the nose.

The ironic thing is that I catch myself using "the voice," on others when I am not getting my way. I am ashamed to say I will use it if I think being a bully will help me quickly achieve my goal. The strange thing is that it usually backfires, and instead of achieving my goal, I encounter a passive resistance.

One of the more effective people I know is a man I have gotten to know during my time in the Rotary Club. His name is Stanley Goldstein. He has a gentlemanly attitude and demeanor. I notice people respond positively to him and think it is in large part due to this trait.

He asks politely and when people resist he backs off and goes in another direction. The thing I noticed is that once people witness his soft answers and gentlemanly ways they do not want to resist his requests even when it means doing something they had rather not do. What a great model of effective leadership!

Recently I ran across a story told by Terry Dobson, a fourth-degree black belt in Aikido, about an encounter he had while riding the subway in Tokyo. It tells beautifully the power of words softly spoken.

A turning point came in my life one day on a train in the suburbs of Tokyo, in the middle of a drowsy spring afternoon. The old car clanked and rattled over the rails. It was comparatively empty—a few housewives with their kids in tow, some old folks out shopping, (and) a couple of off-duty bartenders studying the racing form. I gazed absently at the drab houses and dusty hedgerows.

At one station the doors opened, and suddenly the quiet afternoon was shattered by a man bellowing at the top of his lungs, yelling violent, obscene, incomprehensible curses. Just as the doors closed, the man still yelling staggered into our car.

He was big, drunk and dirty. He wore laborer's clothing. His front was stiff with dried vomit. His eyes bugged out, a demonic, neon red. His hair was crusted with filth. Screaming, he swung at the first person he saw, a woman holding a baby. The blow glanced off her shoulder, sending her spinning into the laps of an elderly couple. It was a miracle that the baby was unharmed.

The couple jumped up and scrambled toward the other end of the car. They were terrified. The laborer aimed a kick at the retreating back of the old lady. "YOU OLD WOMAN!" he bellowed, 'I'LL KICK YOUR %&%!"

He missed; the old woman scuttled to safety. This so enraged the drunk that he grabbed the metal pole in the center of the car, and tried to wrench it out of its stanchion. I could see that one of his hands was cut and bleeding. The train lurched ahead the passengers (were) frozen with fear. I stood up.

I was young and in pretty good shape. I stood six feet, and weighed 225. I'd been putting in a solid eight hours of Aikido training every day for the past three years. I liked to throw and grapple. I thought I was tough. Trouble was my martial skill was untested in actual combat. As students of Aikido, we were not allowed to fight.

My teacher, the founder of Aikido, taught us each morning that the art was devoted to peace. "Aikido," he said again and again, "is the art of reconciliation. Whoever has the mind to fight has broken his connection with the universe. If you try to dominate other people, you are already defeated. We study how to resolve conflict, not how to start it."

I listened to his words. I tried hard. I wanted to quit fighting. I even went so far as to cross the street a few times to avoid the chimpira, the pinball punks who lounged around the train stations. They'd have been happy to test my martial ability. My forbearance exalted me. I felt both tough and holy. In my heart of hearts, however, I was dying to be a hero. I wanted a chance, an absolutely legitimate opportunity whereby I might save the innocent by destroying the guilty.

"This is it!" I said to myself as I got to my feet. "This slob, this animal, is drunk and mean and violent. People are in danger. If I don't do something fast, somebody will probably get hurt. I'm gonna take him to the cleaners."

Seeing me stand up, the drunk saw a chance to focus his rage. "AHA!" he roared, "A FOREIGNER! YOU NEED A LESSON IN JAPANESE MANNERS!" He punched the metal pole once to give weight to his words.

I held on lightly to the commuter-strap overhead. I gave him a slow look of disgust and dismissal. I gave him every bit of nastiness I could summon up.

I planned to take this turkey apart, but he had to be the one to move first. And I wanted him mad, because the madder he got the more certain my victory. I pursed my lips and blew him a sneering, insolent kiss. It hit him like a slap in the face. "ALL RIGHT!" he hollered, "YOUR GONNA GET A LESSON." He gathered himself for a rush at me. He'd never know what hit him.

A split-second before he moved, someone shouted "HEY!" It was ear splitting. I remember being hit by the strangely joyous, lilting quality of it—as though you and a friend had been searching diligently for something, and he had suddenly stumbled upon it. "HEY!"

I wheeled to my left, the drunk spun to his right. We both stared down at a little old Japanese (man). He must have been well into his seventies, this tiny gentleman, sitting there immaculate in his kimono and hakama.

He took no notice of me, but beamed delightedly at the laborer, as though he had a most important, most welcome secret to share. "C'mere," the old man said in an easy vernacular, beckoning to the drunk, "C'mere and talk with me." He waved his hand lightly. The big man followed, as if on a string.

He planted his feet belligerently in front of the old gentleman, and towered threateningly over him. "TALK TO YOU," he roared

above the clacking wheels, "WHY SHOULD I TALK TO YOU?"
The drunk now had his back to me. If his elbows moved so much
as a millimeter, I'd drop him in his socks.

The old man continued to beam at the laborer. There was not
a trace of fear or resentment about him. "What'cha been
drinking?" he asked lightly, his eyes sparkling with interest. "I
BEEN DRINKING SAKE," the laborer bellowed back, "AND
IT'S NONE OF YOUR BUSINESS!" Flecks of spittle spattered
the old man.

"Oh, that's wonderful," the old man said with delight,
"absolutely wonderful! You see, I love sake too. Every night, me
and my wife (she's 76, you know), we warm up a little bottle of
sake and take it out into the garden, and we sit on the old wooden
bench that my grandfather's first student made for him.

We watch the sun go down, and we look to see how our
persimmon tree is doing. My grandfather planted that tree, you
know, and we worry about whether it will recover from those ice
storms we had last winter.

Persimmons do not do well after ice storms, although I must
say that ours has done rather better than I expected, especially
when you consider the poor quality of the soil.

Still, it is most gratifying to watch when we take our sake and
go out to enjoy the evening—even when it rains!" He looked up at
the laborer, eyes twinkling, happy to share his delightful
information.

As he struggled to follow the intricacies of the old man's
conversation, the drunk's face began to soften. His fists slowly
unclenched. "Yeah," he said slowly, "I love persimmons, too...
His voice trailed off. "Yes," said the old man, smiling, "and I'm
sure you have a wonderful wife."

"No," replied the laborer, "My wife died." He hung his head.
Very gently, swaying with the motion of the train, the big man
began to sob. "I don't got no wife, I don't got no home, I don't
got no job, I don't got no money, I don't got nowhere to go. I'm so
ashamed of myself."

Tears rolled down his cheeks, a spasm of pure despair rippled through his body. Above the baggage rack a four-color ad trumpeted the virtues of suburban luxury living.

Now it was my turn. Standing there in my well-scrubbed youthful innocence, my make-this-world-safe-for-democracy righteousness, I suddenly felt dirtier than he was.

Just then, the train arrived at my stop. The platform was packed, and the crowd surged into the car as soon (as) the doors opened. Maneuvering my way out, I heard the old man cluck sympathetically. "My, my," he said with undiminished delight, "that is a very difficult predicament, indeed. Sit down here and tell me about it."

I turned my head for one last look. The laborer was sprawled like a sack on the seat, his head in the old man's lap. The old man looked down at him with compassion and delight, one hand stroking the filthy, matted head.

As the train pulled away, I sat down on a bench. What I had wanted to do with muscle and meanness had been accomplished with a few kind words.

I had seen Aikido tried in combat, and the essence of it was love, as the founder had said. I would have to practice the art with an entirely different spirit. It would be a long time before I could speak about the resolution of conflict.

I too ended up resolving my conflict with my neighbor in a civil way and in civil tones, though my heart wasn't in it. He could see the offense I held for him in my eyes, I am sure. I am not proud of this, but it allows me to know where I stand spiritually, and makes myself aware of my insecurities and places that need healing.

I hope to grow to be like the old Japanese man on the train, who could see beyond a person's wrath and help to dissolve toxic situations with a soft answer. It takes humility to speak a soft answer, but it increases happiness to all.

Discussion Questions:

1. Have you ever been a witness to a soft answer turning away wrath? Discuss.

2. Have you ever used angry tones only to have others resist you? Do you resist those who use angry tones with you? Discuss.

3. What was the genius of the old man on the train?

4. Is using a gentle tone a form of humility? Why or why not?

Chapter Twenty-Six

Choose Relationships Over

Personal Gain

What does it profit a man to gain the whole world, yet lose his own soul?

– Mk. 8:36

There is a great lesson in humility in Genesis 13 that is often overlooked.

Abraham the great patriarch and his nephew Lot are bursting at the seams with material prosperity. Their flocks and herds are growing to the point that the grazing land could not support them both. Their herdsmen were getting into disputes with each other over the best grazing land. Eventually the situation came to a head and Abraham was faced with a decision.

(It is easy for us to see Abraham's dilemma. Something had to be done because his family business was prospering, but his resources were becoming more and more limited as they grew. It was a real problem that people still face today.

Most people who are in family businesses understand the tension and fragility that working with family can bring. No one relishes the thought of an escalating family feud or the ruin of family harmony. It appears that the only solution for Abraham and Lot was to separate if they were going to be able to sustain their lives and continued growth.)

Abraham is Lot's uncle, a superior position in the family pecking order. Abraham is the defacto leader of the clan because of his family status and his age and because he has been entrusted with the mission from God. It would have been perfectly understandable for Abraham to dictate to Lot the terms of their separation...who goes where and who gets what.

However, Abraham does something quite rare and remarkable in the realm of human relationships. He rises above the baser nature of selfishness and shows his faith in God. It seems that his faith in God leads him to act with humility toward Lot.

The Scripture says in Genesis 13:8–9, "So Abram said to Lot, 'Let's not have any quarreling between you and me, or between your herdsmen and mine, for we are brothers. Is not the whole land before you? Let's part company. If you go to the left, I'll go to the right; if you go to the right, I'll go to the left.'"

Lot looked up and saw that the whole plain of the Jordan was well watered, like the garden of the LORD, like the land of Egypt, toward Zoar. So Lot chose for himself the whole plain of the Jordan and set out toward the east. The two men parted company.

How many times are we confronted with a decision like Abraham and Lot's?

Here we see Abraham doing what is unnatural to most of us, which is humbling himself and deferring to Lot. This was a decision that clearly would affect many others beside Abraham.

He had a wife and servants to think about. He had a promise from God of a son, so he had his son's inheritance to consider. However, Abraham clearly chooses brotherhood and friendship over personal gain and his son's inheritance, and instead puts his faith in God to provide what he needed.

We see Lot do what is natural to human nature, and he chose the best for himself. I don't think we stop to consider that Lot, too, had a decision to make. How would he choose? Would he choose wisely? Would he choose out of self-interest? Did he see this as his opportunity to better himself or even to gain the advantage over Abraham?

I wonder what a different story this may have been for Lot and his family had he went against the natural human inclination to take the best land for himself.

We find out later in the story that the land Lot chose was in the middle of Sodom and Gomorrah, and his decision would turn out disastrous for his entire family. What if Lot would have turned down the right to choose first and given the first choice back to Abraham?

Could Lot have changed history? How could this new narrative have changed our lives as we read of this selfless character, Lot? I am not sure, but I suspect it would have changed history.

I remember a few times I acted like Abraham, but more times when I responded like Lot. I am proud of my Abraham decisions and look back with regret over my Lot decisions.

Why am I proud of my Abraham decisions? Well, because they were decisions to choose brotherhood and friendship over personal gain. I look back on those friendships with great fondness and how my decisions strengthened those bonds of friendships.

The regret I feel over my Lot-like decisions is because my selfish decisions usually drove a wedge between myself and my friend. They were not necessarily foolish or sinful decisions, but the decision to choose personal gain over brotherhood always takes a toll.

I can remember one incident in which I am most proud. I was a young salesman coming to work for a major healthcare company. There was pressure to produce new business and we were coming off a major downturn in the economy. I was offered the job in part due to the recommendation of an old college friend who worked in the same capacity as I would be working. We would both be responsible for bringing in new business within the same territory.

These types of situations remind me of watching nature shows where a pack of lions kill a zebra and the dominant male lion fights off all other lions till he has satisfied his hunger. I was the new guy, the smaller lion, and my friend had dibs on all the major accounts left by the previous sales rep.

Like Abraham, I had a choice to make. I could fight for my right to claim some of these coveted accounts or choose to concede them to my friend and carve out my own niche with smaller prospects. I chose brotherhood and friendship, and my sales flourished as did my relationship with my friend. I have never regretted that decision.

Choosing brotherhood and friendship over personal gain takes humility and can seem like the wrong choice for you and your family. However, the blessings that come from brotherhood and friendship can't be measured in dollars and cents.

To choose brotherhood over personal gain also takes a measure of faith in God to provide for your needs and the needs of your family. I learned again the lesson that God resists the proud and gives grace to the humble.

Discussion Questions:

1. "What does it profit a man to gain the whole world, yet lose his own soul?" What does losing your soul mean to you?

2. Can you think of examples where you were faced with choosing a relationship over personal gain? Discuss.

3. How does it take more faith in God to choose a relationship over financial gain?

4. Can you see how being faced with the kind of decision Abraham and Lot faced could change not only your personal history, but also the history of a family?

Part Four

How Humility will Make you Happier

with your Community

Two are better than one, because they have a good return for their labor: If either of them falls down, one can help the other up. But pity anyone who falls and has no one to help them up.

– Eccl. 3: 9–10 NIV

The community consists of the people we share our time, conversation, neighborhood, city, and now more than ever, our world with. It is our family and friends, coworkers, acquaintances, Facebook and Twitter friends, and even the stranger we acknowledge from down the street.

So many of us are looking for and yearning for a stronger sense of community. This is no doubt the reason social media has become so prevalent so quickly. We instinctively know within that we are meant for community, and when it is not there we feel a sense of loss. We all need a community that adds joy, depth and color to our lives.

There are enemies of community and, thankfully, antidotes to help ward off these natural enemies. In the following chapters we hope to explore both.

Chapter Twenty-Seven

Forgiveness Is the First Step

towards Healing

Choose to Forgive—Forgiveness Changes Everything

If you are offering your gift at the altar and there remember that your brother or sister has something against you, leave your gift there in front of the altar. First go and be reconciled to them; then come and offer your gift.

– Matt. 5:23–24 NIV

I need to forgive somebody today, but I really don't want to. I don't want to because they didn't ask me to forgive them.

Ten minutes later...

Well, you will never guess what I just did. I left the keyboard, went into the next room where Devon was folding clothes and told her I was sorry that I hurt her feelings.

"Please forgive me," I said, and I noticed a little tear.

"I'm sorry, too," she said, and we hugged. "I thought you were mad at me. This is not a good time for me," she said as I kissed her on the cheek.

All is well now and she can stop stewing over a short answer I gave her earlier. I wish I had gone to her sooner.

This has nothing to do with forgiving the person I started out to tell you about, but it reminded me of something I needed to do for Devon's sake. It is harder to forgive someone who does not ask your forgiveness.

We all instinctively know this, but something inside resists offering those simple yet healing words, "I am sorry, I was wrong, please forgive me." The words are simple, but they don't flow easily from a proud heart, a heart that doesn't want to admit how insensitive it has become.

Intuitively, I know the only people that hold anger and hurt against me are the people that love, care and respect me. It is harder to hurt someone deeply that could not care less about you. I know that if someone has the ability to hurt me emotionally, then it is a sign of a caring relationship.

Now that I think about it, it is stupid to allow anyone to stay mad or hurt at me. Unfortunately, there have been times that I have disregarded a friend's feeling and thought, *"They'll get over it"* or *"I was right in the first place"* or *"They are over-reacting"* or *"Why are they making such a big deal over this?"*

Those, my friends, are the thoughts and rationale of a proud heart. Pride is a waste of energy. We expend great mental energy justifying ourselves when a humble apology makes things right and puts us back in the flow of a right relationship.

Jesus made a pretty big deal about forgiveness too. When He taught His disciples how to pray, He said, "Forgive us our trespasses as we forgive those who trespass against us." I have heard some argue that we are not obliged to forgive those who do not ask. I ask myself, *Is this the argument of a proud or a humble heart?*

To forgive someone who doesn't ask is certainly more difficult. It stretches my already weak forgiveness muscle.

Something deep within me resists giving away forgiveness. I naturally like to hold on to an offense like it is credit to be redeemed later. If I give forgiveness easily, it feels like I am giving something for nothing.

Grace is not my basic nature. Requiring that others earn what they get from me is my basic nature.

I believe Jesus knew that it is impossible to hold on to an unforgiving attitude without also holding on to anger and hurt. This reminds me of a recent conversation I had with Devon. It went like this:

"You know who I think is a pretty girl," I said.

"Who?"

"Julie."

"She is pretty," Devon said.

"You know, I can't understand why she has such bad luck with boyfriends."

"She's angry."

"She is, isn't she? About what, I wonder?"

"I don't know, but she is."

"It's easy to tell when people are angry isn't it? Am I angry?"

"A little bit."

"How about Janna?"

"She's angry."

"Robin?"

"She's angry and sad."

"Sharon?"

"You know, I think she is good. She is happy with her life."

"Rebecca's angry," I said, "No I think I would say she is more sad than angry

"Anger eventually makes you sad," Devon said. "They go together."

"They do, don't they? How about Melissa?"

"I think she is hurt. I don't think she is angry or sad. She is just hurt."

"I think you are so right. And it is odd that it seems easy to tell the difference. Do you think we are this transparent? Are you angry?"

"Yeah, a little bit."

"About what?"

"Things aren't like I would like them."

"Who are you mad at?"

"Myself, God, maybe others."

"Me?"

"Maybe."

Being humble enough to forgive others, God and even ourselves may be a big challenge for us. It also may be part of what is standing in our way to being at peace and being happy with ourselves and our lives.

Jesus' emphasis on forgiveness shows He understood how crucial to the human condition it is for us to learn to deal with conflict and offense. I believe He knew that if we are generous in giving away forgiveness to those who have hurt and offended us, then anger and hurt and sadness would go away, too.

If offering the words, "I'm sorry, I was wrong to (fill in the blank), please forgive me," will allow another to release forgiveness, then why would I not humble myself enough to do it? There can be only one answer. The disease of pride has so hardened my heart that it can no longer feel and be moved by compassion for another hurt or offended person.

I can already hear the arguments that come from the disease in my own proud heart. *"I WASN'T WRONG! They should not be offended at me. It was their own fault. They started it. Maybe if they stew in it long enough they will change and see the truth. What they did to me was a lot worse than what I did to them."*

It reminds me of what one of my coaches would say to me as I tried to justify a poor performance in a practice or game. Coach would say, "Any excuse will do, Clay…any excuse will do." I believe it is the same with withholding forgiveness. Just pick any excuse you like. Any excuse for not forgiving or not asking forgiveness will do. They all give the same poor result.

I am not saying that we should say we are wrong, when we do not believe we are wrong, but we can almost always say "I was wrong in not trying to get at a resolution sooner," "My attitude has been wrong," etc.

I made a decision to make it easier for people to forgive me.

I have determined I will not withhold the words, "I am sorry, I was wrong, please forgive me." Neither will I withhold my total self from others simply to punish them for their misdeeds.

I will try to make it easier for others to forgive me because I understand that their unforgiving attitude toward me has an exponential effect on the bigger world around me. I understand it affects and hinders their relationship with God and with other people in their life.

I make this decision and determination and know that I am not man enough to keep it. The Spirit within me calls out even now as I think about the way I talked to my brother only a few weeks ago—how I had withheld myself from him. I hoped he let the point I was trying to make soak in.

I wonder how long it will be before my stinging words subside and our relationship will come back to normal. I wonder if our relationship will come back, or if he even really needs me enough anymore to forgive me. Till now, I had been willing to take that chance. How much longer will I wait?

The disease in my heart has a firm hold. It takes humility to make the first move, but making it makes for a happier person.

Discussion Questions:

1. It is harder to forgive someone who does not ask your forgiveness. Discuss.

2. "'I am sorry, I was wrong, please forgive me.' The words are simple, but they don't flow easily from a proud heart, a heart that doesn't want to admit how insensitive it has become." Can you relate to the author's statement? Discuss.

3. "Intuitively, I know the only people that hold anger and hurt against me are the people that love, care and respect me. It is harder to hurt someone deeply that could not care less about you." Discuss.

4. "Grace is not my basic nature. Requiring that others earn what they get from me is my basic nature." Discuss.

5. "I have determined I will not withhold the words, 'I am sorry, I was wrong, please forgive me.' Neither will I withhold my total self from others simply to punish them for their misdeeds." Discuss.

Chapter Twenty-Eight

I Will Make it Easier for Others to Forgive Me

Father forgive them, for they know not what they do.

– Luke 23:34

I decided to make it easier for people to forgive me by asking their forgiveness. So I began by trying it out on a group of friends I regularly meet for coffee. I decided not to wait till I knew I had offended to ask for forgiveness.

I said to them, "I want to ask you all to forgive me."

One of them simply looked at me and said, "Okay."

Another one said, "What am I forgiving you for?"

I said, "I am not sure, but I am sure that I have done something."

They laughed, but not too loudly, and I realized that at some point, I had offended one or more at some time or other in the course of conversations. And I think they genuinely appreciated hearing the words "forgive me" come out of my mouth.

I try to live in a state of awareness that I have been forgiven much. As I write this, I am endeavoring to follow Jesus' example and to *"Forgive them for they know not what they do."*

My declaration is that I now choose to forgive all the sins that people have or will commit against me. I choose to do this because I know that people do not really understand the magnitude and true impact of what they are doing. I will do this also because I know that forgiveness is like a medicine, and an unforgiving attitude like a cancer.

I make this declaration knowing there will be times when I will feel anger, resentment and unforgiveness toward others. But I will remember this declaration and I believe it will help me move to releasing forgiveness more quickly.

This declaration of forgiveness was not my idea. It is an old idea, but still seems new. The idea comes from Jesus' disciples who proclaimed that Jesus died for the sins of the world. My understanding of their message was that His death paid God's price for all sins committed by people for all of human history both past and yet to come.

One of the last sentences uttered by Christ while enduring a crushing betrayal, brutal lashing, verbal assault and horrendous crucifixion was, *"Father, forgive them, for they know not what they do"* (Luke 23:34 KJV).

My diseased heart always heard His words applying to those guards who had taken part in this heinous crime, but now I know His words were for all mankind, to cure the disease that lives in all of us that is capable of this kind of culpability.

"Forgive them." I believe these were not idle words. And that God did not argue, *"No Jesus, I can't. Not for what they have done. Not for what they will yet do to those I love...to my creation."*

Jesus said, "Forgive them."

And God forgave them, and I am one of them. And yet, I was not yet born, but I was forgiven the sin I was yet to commit, and am yet to commit. This has been a hard concept for me and one that I have not always understood.

I was a Christian for many years before I really understood what Jesus had done for me. Though I say I understand it, I wonder if I really grasp it yet.

After Jesus' famous words to forgive them, He uttered equally famous words:

"It is finished" (John 19:30 NASB).

It was years before I asked, "Finished what...?"

I believe the message of the early disciples was that he finished His mission to pay the price required by God that forgives the sins of humankind.

God gives us an example that can leave little doubt about whether He wants us to forgive before we are asked. For the Bible says that while we were yet sinners, Christ died for us. Before we existed, He made the decision to forgive and to sacrifice for sin. All this before we even thought to ask. To forgive before we are asked is the ultimate act of humility. It is also essential for deep happiness.

Discussion Questions:

1. Why is it so hard to forgive others before they ask for forgiveness?

2. What role does forgiveness play regarding Jesus' mission on the earth?

3. The author said that he had made a decision to forgive people even before they had given him a reason to forgive. How could he be able to do that?

4. The author said, "To forgive before we are asked is the ultimate act of humility." Discuss.

Chapter Twenty-Nine

Happy is the One who Learns to

Love What Is

Learning Acceptance

I know what it is to be in need, and I know what it is to have plenty. I have learned the secret of being content in any and every situation, whether well fed or hungry, whether living in plenty or in want. I can do all this through him who gives me strength.

– Philippians 4:12–13

My sister is one of the happiest people I know. She is married with three grown children and eleven grandchildren scattered around the state.

She keeps her infant grandchild during the week as her daughter and her husband work, and on the weekends she travels at least three hours to relieve her son or other daughter as they have a date or weekend retreat.

She has always said that her favorite job in life was being a mother and now she says being a grandmother is even better. She does what she loves and her focus is always on her children's or grandchildren's lives.

I think her secret is that she enjoys her life the way it is and she is blessed that her expectations and the way her life has unfolded are congruent.

Loving Things the Way they Are

My brother Gary may be the second happiest person I have ever known. He married my sweet sister-in-law a couple of years after college. He works an hour's drive away from home so that he can continue to live in our old home place.

He loves our high school and is a savant at remembering high school and college football statistics. He is an elder in the church where we grew up and has stayed faithful to his beliefs. He is a humble person.

He worries about me. He worries that I am not married and have no children. He thinks that is sad and that I too must be sad. He dropped by to tell me this today. To tell me how happy he is. How God answered his prayer that our mother suggested he pray at age 16. To pray for a wife and how God answered that and how that has made all the difference in his happiness.

I appreciate his heart and his concern for me, but I said to him, "I know lots of people who are married with children, but are not happy. Some of them are miserable. Are you sure this makes everyone happy or is it simply why you are happy?

"Daddy Mize (our grandfather) used to tell me, 'Clay, I have always gotten everything I ever wanted.' Then he added, 'But I always knew what to want.' I think he meant that he had the wisdom not to waste his time wanting what he couldn't have or didn't have, but that he had learned to want what he had."

"I think that sometimes we find ourselves with something we didn't expect and are not sure what to do with it. How we handle

159

those unexpected twists and turns in our life can make or break our happiness," I said.

Gary shook his head thoughtfully and said, "That sounds right."

I agree that Gary's wife Linda and his children Emily and Judson add a great deal to his happiness, but I think even more, he is happy because he wants what he has.

He has learned the great lesson of loving things the way they are. Loving things the way they are is an ultimate expression of trust. Like most people who are happy, he is happy without a full understanding of why.

I am not implying that we should always be satisfied with every circumstance we find ourselves in or be passive about making improvements and changes, but I am saying that we should be happy in the moment and trust that even the most egregious circumstances can build something positive in us or benefit someone else.

An unhappy person always wants what they do not have and always has what they don't want, but a humble person loves things the way they are in the moment and accepts that they are that way for a good reason.

Discussion Questions:

1. The author says about his sister, "I think her secret is that she enjoys her life the way it is and is blessed that her expectations and the way her life has unfolded are congruent." Discuss.

2. The author said his grandfather used to make the statement, "I have always gotten everything I ever wanted," but then he added, "But I always knew what to want." Discuss.

3. Loving things the way they are in the moment is an ultimate expression of trust. Discuss.

4. "An unhappy person always wants what they do not have and has what they don't want, but a humble person loves things the way they are and accepts that they are that way for a good reason." Discuss.

5. Why is accepting things as they are an expression of humility?

Chapter Thirty

An Attitude of Service can Make

you Happy

Choose to Serve

Each of you as a good manager must use the gift that God has given you to serve others.

– I Pet. 4:10 GWT

A good technique I have found for shooing away the blues is to see my daily activities in light of how they are of service to others. This too takes the focus off myself and puts my focus on being of service to others.

Many of the things we do each day can be seen as self-serving, but they can also be viewed in light of service to benefit others. By recognizing how our actions benefit others, it triggers a new way of thinking that is healthy for the mind.

The Power of Humility

My old list of chores and routines look like this:

- ✓ Go to the Boxcar café for breakfast.
- ✓ Stop by Food World and pick up a few groceries.
- ✓ Mow the lawn on my rental property.
- ✓ Pay Elaine for cleaning my house.
- ✓ Tie up the tomato plants.
- ✓ Write chapter in book.
- ✓ Meet Mark for lunch.
- ✓ Pay traffic ticket.

My list of activities for June 19th looked like this:

- ✓ Serve the Boxcar restaurant and Gloria the waitress by having breakfast there.
- ✓ Contribute to Food World and to our local economy and jobs.
- ✓ Mow the lawn on my rental property, since my new tenant Wanda will be strapped for time while moving in.
- ✓ Work alongside Elaine who cleans my house. This will make her time go by faster and my paying her will help pay her families expenses.
- ✓ Tie up the tomato plants for Devon.
- ✓ Write chapter about serving others to provide perspective for all who will eventually read it.

✓ Go to lunch with Mark and let our conversation refresh and encourage him.

✓ Serve local law enforcement through contributing to the police department by paying the ticket for my traffic violation.

It may sound silly as you read these things, but listing them this way gives me a totally new perspective and makes doing the routine and mundane more joyful as I see how it all serves the big picture.

Having an attitude of serving others adds perspective and is one of the attitudes of a humble person that leads to a happier life.

Discussion Questions:

1. "A good technique I have found for shooing away the blues is to see my daily activities in light of how they are of service to others. This too takes the focus off myself and puts my focus on being of service to others." Discuss.

2. The author gives a unique way of looking at his "to do" list. Name some regular chores on your "to do" list and see how they can also be of service to others. Discuss.

3. How does getting your mind off yourself and serving others help with your mood and your happiness?

4. Name two ways that you enjoy serving?

<u>Chapter Thirty-One</u>

Happiness is Living in Community

with Others

Put Forth the Effort and Planning to Create a Great Community

Don't just pretend to love others. Really love them. Hate what is wrong. Hold tightly to what is good. Love each other with genuine affection and take delight in honoring each other.

– Rom. 12:9–10 NLT

*O*ne day I pulled in my driveway as usual and I noticed two squad cars and a half dozen unfamiliar cars at the house two doors down. Curious, I walked over to get a little better look and I saw a familiar face.

"William, what is going on?"

166

"They just discovered Bill has died."

"Oh really! What happened?"

"They think he had a heart attack. The coroner thinks that he has been dead for over a week."

"Oh man. That's horrible!"

"Yeah, I think the smell is already pretty bad in there."

"Does he have any family?"

"Yeah, he has a brother that lives in Tennessee. He has been notified."

"No family nearby?"

"Not that I know of."

I turned and walked back home. A pang of guilt hit me. "I am a terrible neighbor," *I thought. If William had not said Bill's name, I would not have known it.*

That might be understandable, except that Bill had been my neighbor two doors down for over 20 years. I had seen the heavyset older man go to his car many times over the years, but he did not get out much other than to leave in his car. I had never introduced myself nor had he. We both lived in relative isolation from one another, though we lived only yards apart for 20 years.

This episode hit me hard and I decided that day to try to do something about it. I called Shevelia, my childhood friend who lived in the neighborhood, and told her the story. We decided to start a neighborhood book club and invite the neighbors to a potluck dinner.

We printed flyers, announced we would study Rick Warren's book, *A Purpose-Driven Life,* and together we canvassed the neighborhood. That was eight years ago.

Though I have since moved out of that neighborhood, we have had a continuous meeting once a week with our book club. It has been a true joy in my life and has provided fellowship for many others. We have had many people come and go, and many friendships developed through the group.

We have shared many Thanksgiving and Christmas dinners, celebrated the marriage of four of our members and supported some as they endured hardships with health issues, teenage issues, divorces and even the death of two members.

I just got off the phone minutes ago to hear about the death of Agnes, one of our first members, who was 96 years old. Shevelia was with her during the last week of her life.

Our club has not been without conflict. There have been times when hurt feelings needed to be mended and other times when members decided to go their separate ways, but overall we developed a community with all its good and bad issues.

Most of all it has been a vehicle for keeping us plugged in to one another and working as a tether to keep us from feeling the isolation that our busy society can create.

To stay in community with others takes humility, because when we are in community, things do not always go the way we think they should. We have to be willing to face those we are in conflict with, and we must be willing to forgive and forget offenses perceived and real.

Though we must humble ourselves at times, the benefits of being a part of a community almost always outnumber the efforts, and in the end, add to our happiness.

Discussion Questions:

1. The author made the following statement about his neighbor. "We both lived in relative isolation from one another, though we lived only yards apart for 20 years." Discuss.

2. What communities do you belong to, i.e., church, civic club, etc.? What things have you done to create a greater sense of community?

3. The author makes the following statement about his book club community. "Most of all it has been a vehicle for keeping us plugged in to one another and working as a tether to keep us from feeling the isolation that our busy society can create." Discuss.

4. What kind of event could you begin planning today that would add to the happiness of your community?

5. How does being a part of a close community help you to stay humble?

Chapter Thirty-Two

We Spread Happiness when We Acknowledge Others

Choose to be Friendly

A man that hath friends must show himself friendly.

– Prov. 18:24a KJV

My friend and Pastor Mark Maybrey invited me to lunch and to meet his friend Ricardo Mia, and by the end of lunch, I was planning a trip to Brazil!

Some people have a way of making you feel at ease—making you feel that you can trust them. Ricardo is one of those people. Part of his friendliness is a natural result of the Brazilian culture.
Ricardo is always touching and hugging you and getting in your space, and he is always doing it with a big smile. He reminds

me of Johnny, my yellow Labrador. I must admit I do not always appreciate Ricardo's overt affection (it's a cultural thing), but I cannot help but like him.

My church supports Ricardo in Belo Horizonte, Brazil, and I was invited to have lunch to meet him and get to know about his work in Brazil. By the end of lunch he looked at me and said, "Clay, my new friend, you should come and visit with me in Brazil. You will love Brazilians."

"Okay," I said. "When can I come?"

"Ricardo, you know Clay is not kidding," Mark, our host, said.

"Neither am I," Ricardo said, and immediately we began to plan my trip.

My trip to Brazil was a great experience for me. I was able to visit the beaches in Rio and go to the Christ statue that overlooks the city. I met many people and visited many of the small house churches. The people were dear, and I appreciated the way they made me feel special.

To be Ignored by Others Chips Away at Our Soul

However, my number one takeaway from the trip was how friendly most people are in the Brazilian cities. It seems that most city dwellers in America keep their eyes straight ahead and try to avoid all eye contact.

In Brazil, it was just the opposite. Ricardo was continually speaking to strangers and initiating conversations wherever we went. While driving, we picked up hitchhikers, and Ricardo honked his horn and waved at everyone we passed.

We acknowledge what we value. It seems to me that we have forgotten the value of a soul. Out of either fear or preoccupation with our own lives, we ignore so many that brush up against our lives. We choose not to acknowledge others. When I need a dose of perspective to remember just how important people are in my life, I reread one of my favorite poems written by Myra Brooks Welch (*The Touch of the Master's Hand*):

Twas battered and scarred, and the auctioneer thought it scarcely worth his while;

To waste much time on the old violin, but held it up with a smile;

"What am I bid, good folks," he cried, "Who'll start the bidding for me?"

"A dollar, a dollar; then two!" "Only two? Two dollars, and who'll make it three?

Three dollars, once; three dollars twice; going for three..." But no,

From the room, far back, a gray-haired man came forward and picked up the bow;

Then, wiping the dust from the old violin, and tightening the loose strings,

He played a melody pure and sweet as a caroling angel sings.

The music ceased, and the auctioneer, with a voice that was quiet and low,

Said; "What am I bid for the old violin?" And he held it up with the bow.

"A thousand dollars, and who'll make it two? Two thousand! And who'll make it three?

"Three thousand, once, three thousand, twice, and going and gone," said he.

The people cheered, but some of them cried, "We do not quite understand;

What changed its worth?" Swift came the reply: "The touch of the master's hand."

And many a man with life out of tune, and battered and scarred with sin,

Is auctioned cheap to the thoughtless crowd, much like the old violin,

A "mess of pottage," a glass of wine; a game—and he travels on.

"He is going once, and going twice, He's going and almost gone."

But the Master comes, and the foolish crowd never can quite understand;

The worth of a soul and the change that's wrought by the touch of the Master's hand.

This reminds me of the story of Zacchaeus, *the wee little man in the Bible. He was despised as a crook by most, but Jesus had the political courage and the spiritual insight to see the value in this little man, who took the initiative to climb a tree to see Jesus.*

Jesus acknowledged him and honored him by requesting to have dinner in his home. This acknowledgement from Jesus transformed this little wheeler-dealer. Zacchaeus immediately made a gift of half that he owned to the poor and promised to repay fourfold to any he had cheated in the past.

Did Jesus use supernatural power to know Zacchaeus would respond in this way, or did he simply have the gift of seeing the best, and acknowledging the best in others?

I do not know if Jesus was using Holy Spirit discernment or if he simply had the disposition to see the best, but either way the outcome was to see the best in others! Best of all, this gift is within all our reach, if we will only see with eyes that value others.

To be ignored by others chips away at our soul and our feelings of self-worth. To be acknowledged encourages us and makes us feel valuable to the world around us. It takes humility to live with an awareness of others, but it adds to our happiness.

Discussion Questions:

1. Some people have a way of making you feel at ease and that you can trust them. Can you name someone who is like this? Discuss what qualities make them this way?

2. The author made the following statement. "It seems that most city dwellers in America keep their eyes straight ahead and try to avoid all eye contact. In Brazil, it was just the opposite. Ricardo was continually speaking to strangers and initiating conversations wherever we went." Do you acknowledge others or simply treat them as objects?

3. We acknowledge what we value. It seems to me that we have forgotten the value of a soul. Discuss.

4. Did Jesus have supernatural power to know Zacchaeus would respond the way he did, or did he simply have the gift of seeing the best, and acknowledging the best in others? Discuss both options.

5. "To be ignored by others chips away at our soul and our feeling of self-worth. To be acknowledged encourages us and makes us feel valuable to the world around us." Discuss.

Chapter Thirty-Three

All Victories are Team Victories

Spread the Credit Around

"There is no limit to what can be accomplished if it doesn't matter who gets the credit."

– Ralph Waldo Emerson

There are No Victories except Team Victories. Nothing can undermine the spirit of a team more than when an individual seeks the credit for a team victory. There are no victories except team victories.

I was fortunate in my youth to be on some winning teams. We were fortunate to have great coaches who implemented the right schemes for our average talent. Though our talent level was average, we made up for it in our desire to be a part of a successful team.

One of the Perils of Success is that It can Spoil You

Thankfully, my teammates and our coaches were quick to help me realize my inadequacies, and I had little opportunity to blow our success into my success. They taught us that when you win as a team, there is plenty of credit and glory to go around. Very few things in life feel better than being a part of a successful team.

Later in life these lessons were invaluable to me as I led a small award-winning staff who would go on to become one of the top employee benefit firms in Alabama. We were also ranked in the top five nationally among one hundred general agencies with a national insurance company.

Fortunately, I was surrounded by talented, hard-working people. Each of our staff members had a strength that the rest of us leaned on.

We had one who was technically savvy, and one who had a gift for dealing with people and making our customers laugh and enjoy doing business with us. We had another who had great organizational skills.

We all depended on one another for our success. The statement that *no one is an island* is true. We needed each other. We needed to work together and we needed to do our job.

My job with our company was leadership. That was the only thing in our organization that I did better than anyone else, and I am proud to say that I was able to find the right people to do jobs better than I could do them myself.

In my estimation, that is the job of a leader. Though I am proud of what we accomplished, I still realize that our function as an organization was only a small cog in a much bigger machine. Lots of people had to work together with a common goal for us to enjoy the success we did.

No One Succeeds Alone

There have been thousands of people who have invested into my life going back to the day when I was just a glimmer in my father's eye. How can you measure that? How can you take credit for who you are?

Yes, we make major decisions in our life about what to do, where to live, who to marry, etc., but the vast majority of the small investments made in us by others just happen. No one orchestrated it, or at least no one human orchestrated it.

How arrogant would it be for me or any of us to take the credit for anything positive that happens in our lives without spreading the credit, and slicing it very thin, so it can go around to all those who made a contribution to the success?

It takes humility to realize that we are just a small cog in a much bigger machine and that we stand on the shoulders of others who have gone before and laid the foundation for the successes we experience.

This thought makes me humble and more appreciative of others like my parents, friends' parents, teachers, ministers, coaches, friends, bosses, coworkers, authors and all those who have invested into my life.

Discussion Questions:

1. "One of the perils of success is that it can spoil you." Discuss.

2. "When you win as a team, there is plenty of credit and glory to go around." Discuss.

3. The author makes the following statement: "I still realize that our function was only a small cog in a much bigger machine. Lots of people had to work together with a common goal for us to enjoy the success we did." Discuss.

4. "There have been thousands of people who have invested into my life going back to the day when I was just a glimmer in my father's eye. How can you measure that? How can you take credit for who you are?" Discuss.

<u>Part Five</u>

How Humility will Make you Happier with your World

For God so loved the world, that he gave his only Son, that whoever believes in him should not perish but have eternal life.

– John 3:16 ESV

How we interact and engage the stranger in our world can impact our own joy and the joy of others. Below are a few characteristics of humble people for you to consider:

> Hospitable, affable, benevolent, congenial, cordial, warm, gracious, pleasant, sociable, open, receptive, neighborly, sincere, sympathetic, welcoming, genuine, concerned, dependable, honest, truthful, trustworthy, credible, plain-spoken, believable,

decent, fair, ethical, reliable, virtuous, mature, safe, and humane.

Practice these and we will make a better world.

<u>Chapter 34</u>

Standing for the Truth with Conviction and Humility Can Change the World

Learn to Know When and How to Stand

For as many as are led by the Spirit of God, they are the sons of God.

– Rom. 8:14

Rosa Parks changed the world. How did she do that, and what did she do? Listen in to an interview at the Academy of Achievement in Williamsburg, VA on June 2, 1995. The bold-face will indicate the interviewer's statements and questions:

"In 1955 you refused to give up your seat to a white passenger on a public bus in Montgomery, Alabama. Your act

inspired the Montgomery bus boycott, the event historians call the beginning of the modern Civil Rights Movement. Could you tell us exactly what happened that day?"

"I was arrested on December 1st, 1955 for refusing to stand up on the orders of the bus driver, after the white seats had been occupied in the front. And of course, I was not in the front of the bus as many people have written and spoken that I was -- that I got on the bus and took the front seat, but I did not.

I took a seat that was just back of where the white people were sitting, in fact, the last seat. A man was next to the window, and I took an aisle seat and there were two women across. We went on undisturbed until about the second or third stop when some white people boarded the bus and left one man standing.

And when the driver noticed him standing, he told us to stand up and let him have those seats. He referred to them as front seats. And when the other three people after some hesitancy stood up, he wanted to know if I was going to stand up, and I told him I was not. And he told me he would have me arrested. And I told him he may do that. And of course, he did.

"He didn't move the bus any further than where we were, and went out of the bus. Other people got off—didn't any white people get off—but several of the black people got off.

"Two policemen came on the bus and one asked me if the driver had told me to stand and I said, 'Yes.' And he wanted to know why I didn't stand, and I told him, 'I didn't think I should have to stand up.' And then I asked him, 'Why did they push us around?'

"And he said, and I quote him, 'I don't know, but the law is the law and you are under arrest.'

"And with that, I got off the bus, under arrest."

"Did they take you down to the police station?"

"Yes. A policeman wanted the driver to swear out a warrant, if he was willing, and he told him that he would sign a warrant when he finished his trip and delivered his passengers, and he *would come straight down to the City Hall to sign a warrant against me."*

"Did he do that?"

"Yes, he did."

"Did the public response begin immediately?"

"Actually, it began as soon as it was announced. It was put in the paper that I had been arrested. Mr. E.D. Nixon was the legal redress chairman of the Montgomery branch of the NAACP, and he made a number of calls during the night, calling a number of ministers."

"I was arrested on a Thursday evening, and on Friday evening is when they had the meeting at the Dexter Avenue Baptist Church, where Dr. Martin Luther King, Jr. was the pastor. A number of citizens came (to the police station) and I told them the story, and from then on, it became news about my being arrested.

My trial was December 5th, when they found me guilty. The lawyers, Fred Gray and Charles Langford, who represented me, filed an appeal and, of course, I didn't pay any fine.

We set a meeting at the Holt Street Baptist Church on the evening of December 5th, because December 5th was the day the people stayed off in large numbers and did not ride the bus. In fact, most of the buses, I think all of them, were just about empty with the exception of maybe very, very few people. When they found out that one day's protest had kept people off the buses, it came to a vote, and unanimously, it was decided that they would not ride the buses anymore until changes for the better were made."

"When you refused to stand up, did you have a sense of anger at having to do it?"

"I don't remember feeling that anger, but I did feel determined to take this as an opportunity to let it be known that I did not want to be treated in that manner and that people had endured it far too long. However, I did not have at the moment of my arrest any idea of how the people would react.

"And since they reacted favorably, I was willing to go with that. We formed what was known as the Montgomery Improvement Association on the afternoon of December 5th. Dr. Martin Luther King, Jr. became very prominent in this movement, so he was chosen as a spokesman and the president of the Montgomery Improvement Association."

"What are your thoughts when you look back on that time in your life? Any regrets?"

"As I look back on those days, it's just like a dream. The only thing that bothered me was that we waited so long to make this protest and to let it be known wherever we go that all of us should be free and equal and have all opportunities that others should have."

"What personal characteristics do you think are most important to being able to accomplish something?"

"I think it's important to believe in yourself and when you feel like you have the right idea, to stay with it. And of course, it all depends upon the cooperation of the people around. People were very cooperative in getting off the buses.

And from that, of course, we went on to other things. I, along with Mrs. Field, who was here with me, organized the Rosa and Raymond Parks Institute for Self-Development. Raymond, my husband—he is now deceased—was another person who inspired me, because he believed in freedom and equality himself."

"How old were you?"

The Power of Humility

"When I was arrested, I was forty-two years old. There were so many needs for us to continue to work for freedom, because I didn't think that we should have to be treated in the way we were, just for the sake of white supremacy, because it was designed to make them feel superior, and us feel inferior. That was the whole plan of racially enforced segregation."

"What people inspired you when you were a child?"

"My family, I would say, my mother, and my maternal grandparents. I grew up with them.

"My mother was a teacher in a little school, and she believed in freedom and equality for people, and did not have the notion that we were supposed to live as we did, under legally enforced racial segregation. She didn't believe in it."

"How did she impart that to you?"

"Just by her attitude and the way she talked. We were human beings and we should be treated as such."

"She instilled that feeling in you?"

"It was just the way I grew up. Yes, she did. Of course, my grandfather had the same ideas, as well as my grandmother."

"What was their background?"

"Both of them were born before the emancipation, before slavery ended. And they suffered a lot; as children they were in slavery and, of course, after slavery was not that much better, but I guess it was some better. They were farmers in a rural area in Alabama."

"They must have suffered."

"Yes, especially my grandfather."

The Power of Humility

"Was there a teacher who influenced you?"

"My mother was a teacher and I went to the same school where she was teaching. My very first teacher was Miss Sally Hill, and I liked her very much.

In fact, I liked school when I was very young, in spite of the fact that it was a one-room school for students of all ages, from the very young to teens, as long as they went to school. It was only a short term for us, five months every year, instead of the regular nine months every year."

"What was it like in Montgomery when you were growing up?"

"Back in Montgomery during my growing up there, it was completely legally enforced racial segregation, and of course, I struggled against it for a long time. I felt that it was not right to be deprived of freedom when we were living in the Home of the Brave and Land of the Free.

Of course, when I refused to stand up, on the orders of the bus driver, for a white passenger to take the seat, and I was not sitting in the front of the bus, as so many people have said, and neither were my feet hurting, as many people have said. But I made up my mind that I would not give in any longer to legally imposed racial segregation, and of course my arrest brought about the protests for more than a year.

And in doing so, Dr. Martin Luther King, Jr. became prominent because he was the leader of our protests along with many other people. And I'm very glad that this experience I had then brought about a movement that triggered across the United States and in other places."

"What would you like to tell us about your life since the bus boycott?"

The Power of Humility

"I would have to take longer than a minute to give my whole synopsis of my life, but I want to let you know that all of us should be free and equal and have equal opportunity, and that is what I'm trying to instill, and encourage and inspire young people to reach their highest potential."

"Tell us about the goals of the Parks Institute."

"We work with young people, from the ages of 11 to 17. Our main program is the Pathways to Freedom. And we'll be going from Memphis, Tennessee, through ten other states, and Washington, DC, and to Canada. It began July 13th and ends August 8th.

We hope to take as many young people and their chaperons as possible throughout these areas, and stop and have workshops and programs. They'll be traveling in buses, and we hope that will inspire and give them a sense of history and also encourage them to be concerned about themselves and history and be motivated to reach their highest potential.

We always encourage them to have a spiritual awareness, because I feel that with the spirit within and our belief in ourselves and our faith in God that we will overcome many obstacles that we could not with negative attitudes.

I want to always be concerned with being positive, and them being positive and believing in themselves, and believing that they should be good citizens and an asset to our country and for the world. And I believe in peace too, and not violence."

"What does the American Dream mean to you?"

"I think the American Dream should be to have a good life, and to live well, and to be a good citizen. I think that should apply to all of us. That it is the Land of the Free and the Home of the Brave, and I believe it should be just that for all people, who can think of themselves as human beings and that they will enjoy the blessings of the freedom of this country."

"Are we moving as quickly as you might like in that direction?"

"We still have a long way to go; we still have many obstacles and many challenges to face. It's far from perfect, and it may never be, but I think as long as we do the best we can to improve conditions, then people will be benefited."

"You don't get negative about the negative things?"

"No, I don't. I try to not think of those things that we cannot control, but I think if we continue to work with positive attitudes, conditions will be better for more people."

"What advice would you give to a young person who wants to make a difference?"

"The advice I would give any young person is, first of all, to rid themselves of prejudice against other people and to be concerned about what they can do to help others. And of course, to get a good education, and take advantage of the opportunities that they have.

In fact, there are more opportunities today than when I was young. And whatever they do, to think positively and be concerned about other people, to think in terms of them being able to not succumb to many of the temptations, especially the use of drugs and substances that will destroy the physical health, as well as mental health."

"What would you say to a kid who's in trouble now?"

"The reason we start with them so young is to try to get them a good family life, before they get into that area. Of course there are those who maybe have strayed away, and I would certainly advise them to find some means of helping themselves, even if they've gotten into some problems."

"Family is important to you."

"Yes, it is, very important. Of course, we have so many broken homes now. Young people need some means of being encouraged and trying to find some role models—people in school, in church, and in other organizations. They need to be organized to work together, instead of being so scattered about and not having any positive outlook on life."

"Did you feel Dr. King had a special gift?"

"Well, when I first met him it was before I was arrested. I met him in August of 1955, when he came to be the guest speaker at an NAACP meeting and I was secretary. I was very impressed with his delivery as a speaker and, of course, his genuine friendliness as a person. And his attitude, of course, was to work and do whatever he could in the community for the church to make a difference in the way of life we had at that time.

And I was really impressed by his leadership, because he seemed to be a very genuine and very concerned person, and, I thought, a real Christian."

"Did it surprise you when he became a national hero?"

"No, not really, because I just felt that he filled the position so well. He was the type of person that people really gravitated towards and they seemed to like him personally, as well as his leadership."

"Was he a warm person?"

"Yes, he was."

"It has been an honor to sit with you here, today. Thank you so much for spending this time with us, Mrs. Parks.

The Power of Humility

Rosa Parks stood up for her convictions with humility. She was ready to receive the consequences for what she knew was an unrighteous law.

She didn't put a bomb on the bus like some do today who are trying to impose their agenda on everyone else. She stood for what she believed in without violence, and her humble, yet courageous action stirred up the righteous indignation of others—and the modern-day Civil Rights Movement was born.

Rosa's simple act of humbly resisting a despicable law inspired Dr. Martin Luther King, Jr. to act. King was a man prepared for his moment in history, but he needed the spark provided by Rosa's act of courage and humility.

True Hearts are Ready to be Set Ablaze

What others have gathered inspiration and courage from Dr. King? This question is almost too big to fathom. To follow is a few documented acts sparked by Rosa's courage, but it is the millions of undocumented acts of courage that have provided exponential results. The following are a few we know about:

Lech Walesa, the Polish factory worker who stood for the rights of Polish workers against the domineering Soviet regime, has given King some credit for his inspiration.

It was Lech Walesa's courage that inspired Mikhail Gorbachev, the Soviet President to implement changes of Perestroika (restructuring) and Glasnost (Openness) which paved the way for freedoms for the Soviet people that changed the lives of millions.

Nelson Mandela was fighting a similar battle to Dr. King's in South Africa. Mandela served a twenty-five-year prison sentence for his efforts to end Apartheid, a segregation policy similar to what Dr. King faced in Alabama. Finally, Mandela too prevailed and ascended to the presidency of South Africa.

When he stood to accept the Nobel Peace Prize in 1993, nearly thirty years after Dr. King had received his, Mr Mandela recalled the American's words when he said: "Let the strivings of us all prove Martin Luther King, Jr. to have been correct, when he said that humanity can no longer be tragically bound to the starless midnight of racism and war."

Aung San Suu Kyi, sometimes called Burma's Ghandi, fights even today a similar fight in Burma. After being elected president in 1990, the election was annulled by the military six days later, and she was in detention for over twenty years because of her fight for independence and freedom for the Burmese people.

She has suffered greatly in that she had grandchildren she has never seen. She too says her inspiration for non-violent resistance to unjust laws comes from both Mandela and King.

Although Dr. King was both inspirational and effective in fanning this flame, he too gathered his inspiration from others. Much of the inspiration King claimed came from studying the methods of Gandhi in India.

Gandhi's non-resistant methods have been a model for many others in their struggles for their people. Gandhi stood against the exploitation of British Colonialism to bring freedom to India.

Gandhi too claimed to have inspiration. He credited Leo Tolstoy, the Russian poet and novelist, for some of his inspiration. Gandhi and Tolstoy corresponded frequently. Tolstoy, who converted to Christianity later in life, regularly shared his gleanings with Gandhi regarding Jesus' Sermon on the Mount. Gandhi, though a Buddhist, acknowledged his inspiration for non-violent resistance came from Jesus' sermon.

There was no example of non-violent resistance, before the example of Jesus. He stood up to the tyranny and hypocrisy of King Herod and the corrupt religious elite who were oppressing and gouging the poor.

What greater illustration of a non-violent protest than the day He was crucified! The prophecies of Isaiah came true in Jesus. Isaiah said about the coming Messiah, "He was oppressed and afflicted, yet he did not open his mouth; he was led like a lamb to the slaughter, and as a sheep before its shearers is silent, so he did not open his mouth" (Isaiah 53:7).

Peter, speaking about that day said, "When they hurled their insults at him, he did not retaliate; when he suffered, he made no threats. Instead, he entrusted himself to him who judges justly" (I Peter 2:23).

Jesus' fire has never burned as brightly as it does today. The Kingdom advances. He still inspires. Over 3 billion people worldwide claim Jesus the Christ as their spiritual leader. Even Communist China, a country who has tried to contain and restrict His movement, has eclipsed the U.S. as having more individuals who claim to be Christ's followers.

Seekers around the world are coming to recognize Jesus as the great liberator. He is the One recognized as standing for the little guy...the powerless. He endured what the depraved had in store for those who stand against them, so that those with eyes to see, would also find within themselves the courage to stand.

Though we may never be called on to make such a dramatic stand against injustice as Jesus or King or Gandhi, we will probably be confronted with an opportunity to stand against injustice in a hundred smaller ways.

Are we prepared? Are we allowing God to strengthen our character in order that we can stand when we are called upon?

To make a stand with humility like Jesus did, and the others in this chapter, can change the world, and make it a happier place for everyone.

Discussion Questions:

1. "Rosa's simple act of humbly resisting a despicable law inspired Dr. Martin Luther King, Jr. to act. King was a man prepared for his moment in history, but he needed the spark provided by Rosa's act of courage and humility." Discuss.

2. "What greater illustration of a non-violent protest than the day He was crucified! The prophecies of Isaiah came true in Jesus. Isaiah said about the coming Messiah, 'He was oppressed and

afflicted, yet he did not open his mouth; he was led like a lamb to the slaughter, and as a sheep before its shearers is silent, so he did not open his mouth' (Isaiah 53:7)." Discuss.

3. "Jesus' fire has never burned as bright as it does today. The Kingdom advances. He still inspires. Over 3 billion people worldwide claim Jesus the Christ as their spiritual leader. Even Communist China, a country who has tried to contain and restrict His movement, has eclipsed the U.S. as having more individuals who claim to be Christ's followers." Discuss.

4. "Though we may never be called on to make such a dramatic stand against injustice as Jesus or King or Gandhi, we will probably be confronted with an opportunity to stand against injustice in a hundred smaller ways." Discuss.

Your Next Step

Now that you can see how the power of humility can change your life, it is time for the next step by reinforcing these ideas with you and your team. How can you do this? There are a number of ways. Here are some of them.

- Invite Clay to visit your church, business, school or organization to speak to your team about the transformational benefits of humility. (See the next page for details)
- Share your story with us how an aspect of humility has changed your life. Some of the very best stories we will share with our followers on our weekly blog and who knows maybe our next book. Go to our website at www.claymize.com
- Follow Clay's blog. Go to www.claymize.com and click the subscribe button and you will get periodic updates of Clay's stories and insights about humility.
- Give us a book review. Go to our www.claymize.com and post your comments how The Power of Humility, The Powerful Secret that will make you Happy and Change the World has given you new perspective
- Visit our facebook page at www.facebook.com/ClayJMize

Embark on a life changing journey and experience how choosing humility causes God's favor to be upon you!

Clay Mize

Bring Clay Mize to your organization. He is available for:

- Seminars on a wide variety of topics
- Conferences or educational events
- Consulting with your organization

For other resources or dates of seminars and workshops visit:

www.ClayMize.com

To contact Clay to speak to your organization send email to:

Claiborne.Mize@gmail.com

About the Author

Clay's career began at age seven on his grandfather's farm raising chickens and learning the meaning of a long row to hoe.

Two turning points in Clay's life was trying out for quarterback and attending the University of Alabama. The first gave him the confidence that he could be a leader and the other plucked him from the safety of his home town.

In the years following Clay worked as a furniture assembler, lifeguard, paper boy, waiter, cookie salesman, oil field roustabout, teacher, and talk show host. More recently he worked in entrepreneurial ventures in insurance, real estate and coaching.

Clay has developed curriculum that he uses to coach business owners and managers as well as university students. A sample of courses offered to organizations include;

- The Power of Humility to Build Your Team
- Relationship Marketing
- Finding your True Purpose
- Secrets to Business Success
- Asking the Right Questions, How Great Businesses Stay Out Front of the Competition

For more seminars and workshops or to book Clay to speak to your organization email him at Claiborne.Mize@gmail.com

Made in the USA
Charleston, SC
24 December 2013